KANSAS SCHOOL OF RELIGION
UNIVERSITY OF KANSAS
1300 OREAD AVENUE
LAWRENCE, KANSAS 66044

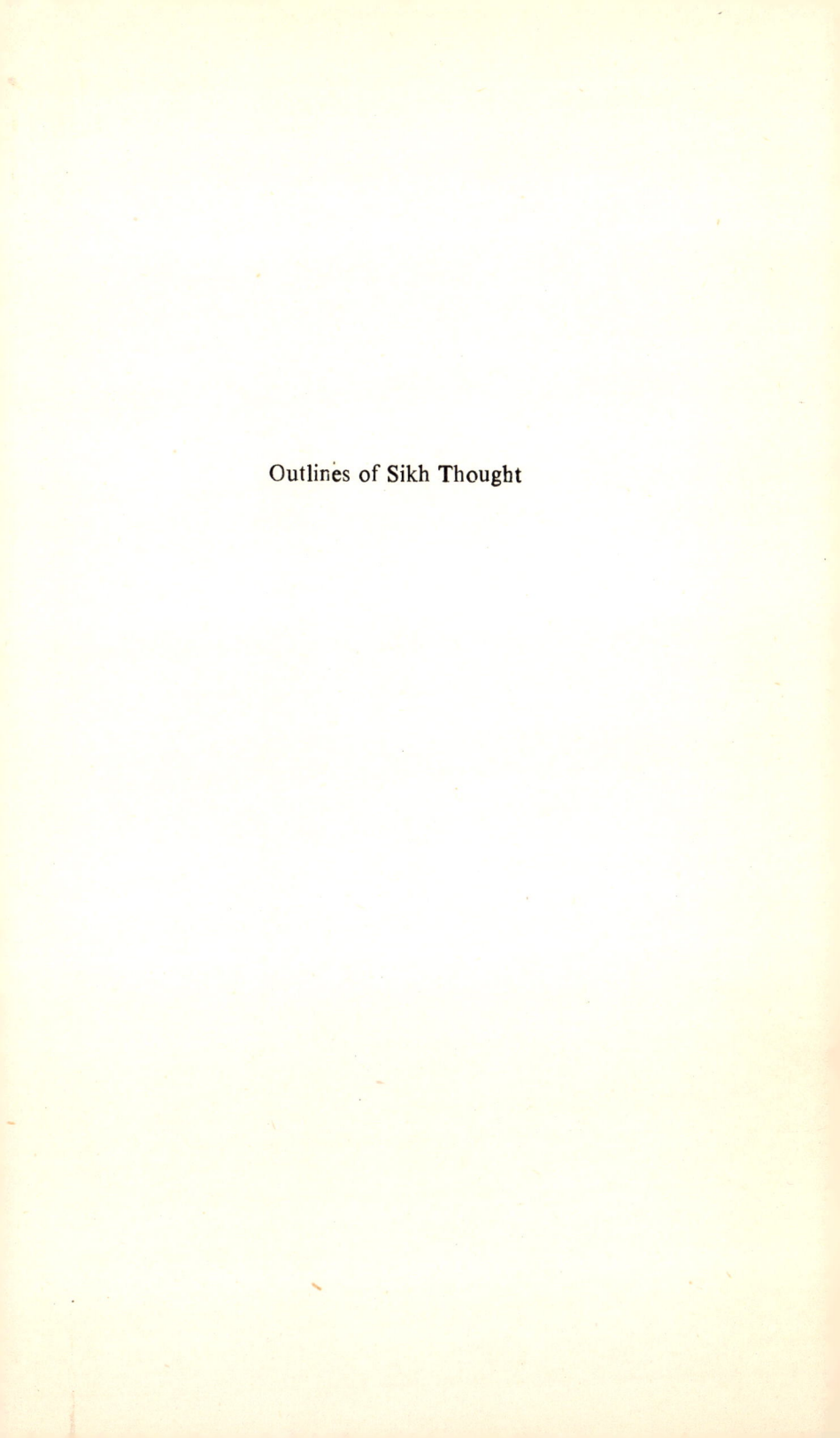

Outlines of Sikh Thought

Outlines of Sikh Thought

by
Dr. Surindar Singh Kohli

Munshiram Manoharlal
Publishers Pvt. Ltd.

Sikhism

Second revised edition 1978
© 1976 **Kohli**, Surindar Singh

Published by
Munshiram Manoharla
Publishers Pvt. Ltd.
54 Rani Jhansi Road
New Delhi-110055
Printed by
Brother Enterprises
EG-132 Inderpuri
New Delhi-110012

Contents

PREFACE vii

1

Introduction . . . 1
The Adi Granth—Consummation of Indian Culture 3
Philosophy of Sikhism in a Nutshell 10

2

SIKH PHILOSOPHY 16

The Concept of Brahman 16
The Concept of Jiva 22
The Concept of Maya 26
The Concept of Creation 29
Microcosmic Theory as enunciated in the *Adi Granth* 38
The Concepts of Karma and Transmigration 42
The Concepts of Hukm 45
√The Concept of Grace 49
The Concept of Virtue and vice 50
The Concept of Ego 54
The Concept of Mind and Intellect 56
The Concept of Death and Life after Death 59
Notes and References 62

3

SIKH RELIGION 76

The Concept of Heath 76

The Concept of Yoga *79*
The Concept of Bhakti *82*
The Concepts of Satguru and Name *84*
The Concepts of Sadh Sangat and Kirtan *93*
The Concepts of a True Sikh and an Ideal Society *97*
The Sikh Ceremonies *102*
God-Realization *108*
Notes and References *112*

INDEX

Preface

In this short treatise an attempt has been made to elucidate the basis concepts of Sikh religion and philosophy. It is a revised and enlarged edition of the work, first published in 1966. The references from the Sikh scriptures have been given in Devanagri script, so that the students of Comparative Religion in India and abroad may get some acquaintance with the original text.

The treatise has been divided into three parts. The first part is introductory. The second part deals with various concepts of Sikh Philosophy and the third part with concepts of Sikh Religion. The study is, of course, very brief and may be called the quintessence of Sikh religion in theory and practice.

The first edition of the book was well received by the students, scholars and researchers of not only Panjabi literature, but also of religion and philosophy. The work has been frequently quoted in research theses. S. Khushwant Singh, the distinguished writer and scholar, gave the following remarks after studying it, "I am deeply impressed with its clarity and sound scholarship. I have read nothing to equal it and am grateful . . . for making so many points which had baffled me — now appear so simple."

There had been a constant demand for the publication of the second edition of this book. I am thankful to Messrs

Munshiram Manoharlal Publishers Pvt. Ltd. New Delhi for the pains they have taken in bringing out the work in its excellent final form.

Surindar Singh Kohli

Chandigarh.
September, 1977

1

Introduction

Guru Nanak, the founder of Sikhism and high-priets of Indian Mysticism in the Punjab was born in 1469 AD. Nine Gurus succeeded him one after another. The last Guru Gobind Singh passed away in 1708 AD. He did not appoint any human successor and bestowed the Guruship on the *Adi Granth*, which was compiled by Guru Arjan in 1604.

Adi Granth contains the compositions of not only the Sikh Gurus, but also of some prominent Indian Saints including those of Jaidev of Bengal (of 12th century), Farid of West Punjab (of 12th century), Namdev of Maharashtra (of 14th century), Kabir of U.P. (of 15th century) and Ravidas of U.P. (of 15th century). This fact is an ample proof of a religious movement in India, culminating in the Punjab with Guru Nanak and his successors. This movement is known as *Bhakti Movement*.

The compositions of the *Adi Granth* give us a picture of the political, social and religious conditions in India, during the *Bhakti Movement*. The standard of life was at its lowest ebb. The State was negligent in its duties towards its subjects. "The kings were butchers." "Greed was the king and the sin his minister." Under such circumstances, the real Indian culture was forgotten. The Brahmin, the custodian of Hindu society had to please the Muslim ruler, therefore, he could not talk of real Indian heritage freely. He was merely a performer of ceremonies, which brought him material gains. He remembered *mantras* of *Vedas* for performing rituals and worship, but forgot *Vedanta* i.e. *Upanishads* which taught *Para Vidya*.

Two cultures had met, the Hindu culture on one side and Islamic culture on the other. The Hindu was polytheist and the Muslim a monotheist. The Hindu was an idol-worshipper and the Muslim was an idol-breaker. The Hindu was a believer of *Varnashrama Dharma*, while a Muslim believed in a common brotherhood. Therefore, the Hindu and the Muslim were antagonistic to each other. There was great antagonism on the religious plane, therefore, the Hindu was suppressed by the Muslim ruler.

In the Hindu social set-up, the Shudra was the most exploited caste. The Brahmin frowned upon him and made him an untouchable in the society. He was not only a prey to the excesses of *Dvijas*, but the rulers also suppressed him as a Hindu. This annoying situation compelled him to take refuge in the Lord Almighty. There is no doubt that many Shudras found comfort in the fold of Islam, but there were others who enjoyed relief in their surrender to the Lord. There were several of the remarkable saints, who came from this class. Namdev, a calico printer of Maharashtra, Kabir, a weaver and Ravidas, a cobbler of U.P. etc. rose by their devotion to the Lord.

Out of the four *Ashramas* (the stages of life) the *Vanaprasthis* (forest-dwellers) and the *Sannyasis* (religious mendicants) who were supposed to be spiritually advanced people, were far from the real religious life. The *Sannyasis* were "the *Thugs* of Benaras." All types of orthodox and heterodox ascetics were devoid of spiritual values.

The Hindu society was divided into several sects. There were *Vaishnavas*, *Shaivas*, *Shaktas*, *Sauryas* and *Ganapatyas*. They laid more stress on rituals and ceremonies. Their religion had degenerated into symbolism and ritualistic practices.

The Nath cult, which laid emphasis on *Hathyoga*, had become an enormous force to be reckoned with. The Yogis misused the miraculous powers attained by them through *Yoga*. Guru Nanak and his descendants rejected their aloofness and practices.

INTRODUCTION 3

Guru Nanak through his *Goshtas* (conversations) and hymns presented a way of life to the people of the country, preserving their real culture and rejecting the passivity and self-mortification preached by certain sects. The succeeding Gurus elucidated the reformative and revolutionary thought expressed by the first Guru. Although this path of life enunciated by the Sikh Gurus was the product of a definite period of history, its tenets and beliefs belong to all times; its approach is universal.

This short treatise on the Sikh thought has resulted from my innermost desire of bringing before the world the concepts of this youngest of world-religions, which have not been understood and appreciated by the peoples of the world uptil now. I have divided this treatise into two parts *viz*. Sikh Philosophy and Sikh Religion. By the perusal of both these parts one can visualize the significance of the Sikh thought and practice. The Sikh thought and doctrines are universal in character. The Sikhs are standard bearers of liberty, equality and fraternity in the world. They are free from local prejudices and parochial outlook.

The *Adi Granth*, the scripture of the Sikhs, is the source-book for all the thoughts expressed in this book. The reader can make a comparative study of this thought with other systems of Indian and world thought and appreciate the catholicity of views and universalism contained in the doctrines of the Sikh Gurus. I shall deem myself fully rewarded, if this short treatise gives a complete view of Sikh thought and practice to an ordinary reader.

The Adi Granth—Consummation of Indian Culture

The *Adi Granth* is the latest sacred book of Asia. It was compiled by Guru Arjan, the fifth Sikh Guru in 1604. It contains the compositions of not only the Sikh Gurus, but also of some prominent Indian Saints including Jaidev of Bengal (of 12th century), Farid Shakarganj of West Punjab (of 12th-

13th century), Namdev of Maharashtra (of 14th century), Kabir and Ravidas of Uttar Pradesh (of 15th century). These compositions manifest synthesis of Indian Thought, an exposition of the ideal life of an individual and society and a consummation of Indian Culture. The path of life enunciated by the Sikh Gurus and the Saints in the *Adi Granth* is universal in character and common for all humanity.

The Vedic culture is the most important phase in the composite culture of India, when the people led a pastoral life and the basis of their social structure was the family. The state was monarchical and the people expressed their will through popular assemblies *i.e. Samitis*. The caste system which has played a significant part in the making and preservation of Hindu Society, developed during this phase of Indian culture. The Brahmins and Kshatriyas enjoyed the privileged position in the society. The religion was polytheistic. In order to obtain divine favour, rituals and sacrifices were performed. The span of life was divided into four *Ashramas*. The theories of *Karma* and transmigration of souls were evolved during this period.

The four Vedas are basic scriptures of Hinduism. The Vedic seers were gifted with divine vision. Each Veda contains four parts: *Mantra, Brahmana, Aranyaka* and *Upanishad*. The first part contains Mantras or divine hymns. The second part contains the guidelines for the performance of the sacrificial rites and the third part gives philosophical interpretation of the rituals. The last and the fourth part contains metaphysical teachings about the ultimate Reality. Names of several gods are mentioned in Vedic hymns, but a close study of the hymns reveals that there is unity in diversity. The All Pervading *Purusha* appears as Impersonal Absolute in *Nasadiya-Sukta*. The Upanishads are the philosophical treatises, which bring forth clearly the nature of Brahman and the *Atman*, the significance of *Aum* and the relation between the non-dual reality and the world of plurality. They propound two views of reality, the cosmic (*saprapanch*) and the acosmic (*nishprapancha*), the former holding the universe as a real manifestation of Brahman and the later an illusionary appearance of Brahman.

The authority of the Vedas was repudiated by the materialistic Charavaks, Jains and Buddhists. The Charvakas believed that there was no God, no *Atman* and no life hereafter. The Jains and Buddhists accepted the doctrines of *Karma* and rebirth, but revolted against the traditional polytheism and caste system. Jainism is atheistic. Though it denies the existence of God, it believes in Arhats. There is no place of *Bhakti* (or worship) in Jainism. It believes in two categories: *Jiva* and *Ajiva*. The *Jivas* are infinite in number. The *Ajiva* includes *Pudgal* (Matter), *Dharma, Adharma,* Space (*Akasha*) and Time (*Kala*). The *Karmic* particles put the soul in bondage, which can be liberated by following the three Jewels (*Triratna*) of right faith, right knowledge and right conduct. The Buddhists believe in four noble truths and eightfold path. They do not accept the Hindu concept of soul. They oppose the debased form of worship and the spirit behind sacrifices. Jainism and Buddhism both laid emphasis on *Ahimsa*, non-injury to living beings. Both have ascetic orders.

With the rise of Jainism and Buddhism, there was released a new spirit of enquiry and a re-orientation of Hindu Culture. The philosophical and religious ideas of Hinduism were conveyed to the masses through *Itihasas* (*Ramayana* and *Mahabharata*) and *Puranas*. The famous song of the Lord *i.e. Bhagavat Gita* forms part of *Mahabharata*. The six systems of Hindu Philosophy sprang up during this period and there was revival of Hinduism. The caste-system was still the basis of social organisation. The Law Books restricted the freedom of women and thus there was steady deterioration in her status. The King was expected to be guardian of his subjects.

Though Indian Culture was synthetic and absorbed in its fold several dissimilar cultures, but because of sharp contrast, the assimilation of Islam in-toto in Indian Culture could not be possible. There was, however, marked impact of Muslim culture on Indian literature, architecture, music etc. A new mixed language was born and a reformist movement known as *Bhakti Movement* came into being. Kabir and Guru Nanak were its chief exponents at the time of its culmination. They were the high-priests of Indian mysticism. The message of Kabir, Guru Nanak and other Sikh Gurus and Indian Saints was preserved in the *Adi Granth* by the fifth Sikh Guru, Guru Arjan. This holy *Granth* (The Scripture of the Sikhs) was compiled in 1604, and as has been said above, it included the compositions of the holy Gurus and saints ranging from twelfth to seventeenth century.

During his lifetime Guru Nanak had travelled far and wide not only in India but also in various Asian Countries. He studied not only the various phases of Indian Culture minutely, but also the culture of other nations and countries. He held discussions with the leaders of various cultural centres of his time. He had drawn his conclusions regarding an ideal culture and cultured person which are contained in his compositions included in the *Adi Granth*, Guru Arjan studied the cultural heritage of India rendered in the popular tongue and selected the best compositions which responded to Guru Nanak's Concept of Culture. For Guru Nanak Culture not only includes ethical greatness and aesthetic grandeur, but also spiritual achievements. Therefore, the culture preached by Guru Nanak may be called spiritual culture or a culture of eternal values *i.e. Sanatana Dharma*. The *Vedic Dharma* (or *Sanatana Dharma*) attracted his attention because it was also a spiritual culture, but he differed with it on various points.

The *Adi Granth* exhibits before us a Parliament of preceptors and saints, who belonged to various classes and strata of society and who spoke on behalf of all the inhabitants of the universe. Their concern was for *the man*, who may be living anywhere in the world. Their culture took within its compass the whole of humanity, the human beings of all castes, colours and creeds. They called their cultured man '*Gurmukh*,' who was above lust, anger, greed, attachment, ego, indignation, delusion, jealousy, vanity, enmity *etc.* and imbibed the virtues of truth, continence, sweetness, contentment, self-control, modesty, straight-forwardness, compassion, fearlessness, purity, moderation, faith, generosity, humility etc.

The contributors of the *Adi Granth* were inheritors of a vast culture and its limitations. Therefore, they chiselled out the unnecessary material, which had lost its value with the passage of time or which according to the past experience had proved worthless or injurious in any way in the making of an ideal cultured person. They perfected the image of Indian Culture. They did away with the flaws of the existing cultural concepts and brought in the best and workable concepts. They were thus responsible for the consummation of Indian Culture.

THE *ADI GRANTH*—CONSUMMATION OF INDIAN CULTURE

All the gods and *Avataras* (incarnations) were rejected. The Impersonal Absolute does not take birth, therefore, only the Absolute is to be worshipped. The individual who should devote himself whole-heartedly to the All-Pervading, Omnipresent, Omnipotent and Omniscient Lord and should lead a family and social life. The division of the span of Life into *Ashramas* was thus rejected. Emphasis was laid on the life of a house-holder i.e. *Grahasthya Ashrama*. It is of no use to become *Vanaprastha* or a *Sannyasi*. All the ascetic orders were decried. Asceticism exhibits defeatist mentality and passivity. It may lead to several evils and vices. One must work hard to earn his livelihood and not depend upon the mercy of others. Guru Nanak has said, "Those who work hard for their livelihood and give something in charity to the deserving, they only recognise the Path leading torwards the Lord." In this respect, the ideal of a *Karma Yogi* has been set forth. The Individual has not only to perform duties for his self, but also for his family and society. The service of humanity leads us towards the Lord. This is the social aspect of the spiritual culture of the *Adi Granth*. The institution of free kitchen (*langar*) may be mentioned in this connection.

The *Adi Granth* rejects all formalism and ritualism and lays emphasis on the adoption of ethical qualities. The Vedic Seers and the *Bhakti* Cults all stress the necessity of performing rituals, sacraments and sacrifices. They are performed to please gods and win their favour. Such like acts throw into the background the real objective of the human life. Moreover, these acts create ego in the mind of the person, who performs these rites, therefore, they are of no avail. The word '*Samskara*' used for sacrament has often been considered synonymous with culture. A *samskara* is said to re-make one's personality. But the *Adi Granth* does not attach any importance to *samskaras*. It lays emphasis on the qualities of the self (*Atman-Gunas*). Guru Nanak has said of *Upanayana samskara*:

    Let the cotton be of mercy, the thread of contentment,
        the knots of self-control and twists of truth.
    O Pandit: Put on me such *Janeu* of the soul.   *Rag Asa*

Most of the rituals were performed before the idols of gods. The saints of the *Adi Granth* have ridiculed the idea of image-worship. The Impersonal Absolute cannot be installed as an

image. Namdev of Maharashtra says:
"We venerate one stone and pass over the other
If one is god, the other must also be the same."

In the *Adi Granth*, the reality of the world and the significance of the poise and balance in life has been stressed. There is equal stress on the physical and spiritual well-being of individual and society and a balanced combination of knowledge, action and devotion. The individual should take great care of the body, which is a temple of the Lord. But equal care should be taken of the spiritual development. For the health of the body and the spirit, the mind and intellect should also be kept healthy. Any strain on the body for the spiritual development or negligence of spirit for physical health is not advisable. The Yogic practices comprising of *Āsanas* and *Pranayama* are thus not recommended. Kabir says in respect of the body and Cit:

Namdev says to Trilochan, Repeat the Name of the Lord
in the mouth
Do all the work with your hands and feet and keep your
cit absorbed in *Niranjan*.

The *Adi Granth* preaches the fatherhood of God and brotherhood of man. It rejects all barriers and prejudices of caste, colour and birth and lays emphasis on equal status of man and woman in society. It speaks against all types of exploitations. All the distinctions in respect of caste have been decried, because the caste system creates social evils of inequality and untouchability. The different castes are man-made distinctions. In the House of God, all are equal. A Brahmin should be one who realises Brahman; A Kashtriya is one who shows bravery in the field of good actions. Everywhere the human body is composed of earth, air, water and fire, then why should there be distinctions between man and man? Kabir who was a Shudra, has questioned the Brahmin in the following manner:

How you are a Brahmin? How I am a Shudra?
How I am blood and how you are milk?

Guru Nanak has said that the castes should be on the basis of actions and should not be hereditary.

The Law-codes of Hinduism had placed the woman in a very inferior position as compared to man. She was considered evil and impure, though she was the mother and nurse of all men. Guru Nanak said emphatically:

Why should we talk ill of her who gives birth to Kings?

The *Adi Granth* is international and universal in outlook and propagates the idea of one world and one religion. It rises above the restraint of food, clothing etc., but speaks against the use of drugs and intoxicants. That food is debarred which makes the individual insane. The contributors of the *Adi Granth* have laid emphasis on moderation and continence. The excess of indulgence and self-mortification both are considered bad.

The *Adi Granth* talks about the basic needs of individual *i.e.* food, shelter and clothing and lays a great responsibility on the State regarding their provision. The state should be democratic and should work for the well-being and prosperity of individual and society. The individual should work for himself, his family and his state and the state in turn should look after his requirements and those of his family. The starved society cannot experience a spiritual awakening. That state is prosperous, whose individuals perform their duties sincerely and seriously. The Head of the State or the King should be considerate and should always think of the well-being of his people. If the King leads a luxurious life without caring for the well-being of his subjects, his rule will be short-lived and there will be revolution in the State. Guru Nanak has said:

"That King will hold the throne, who has the necessary qualities of kingship and who follows the democratic ideals."

The *Adi Granth* advocates the excellence and utility of human life, the necessity of education, truthful living and true preceptor, the building of character, the inculcation of love, truth, contentment, humility etc. and the achievement of spiritual greatness by following the path enunciated by the preceptor. It is said that even the gods crave for the human body, because it is only through its medium that one can attain final emancipation. The mind and intellect associated with the human body should be given proper education, so that the best of results may be achieved with the proper and balanced combination of body, mind, intellect and soul. All these parts of an individual entity should be looked after simultaneously.

A closer examination of the above-mentioned points in respect of the *Adi Granth*, clearly shows that it expounds the ideal cultured person, in whom all the qualities are enshrined. We may thus conclude that the *Adi Granth* is not only a repository of the essence of great Indian Culture, but also its perfection, completion and consummation.

Philosophy of Sikhism in a Nutshell

The Sikh Philosophy recognises three means of knowledge only *viz.* perception, inference and scriptural testimony. The perception includes the perception of ordinary persons *i.e.* the contact of the soul with the sense-organs and objects through mind, the perception of the 'Liberated souls' *e.g.* of the Guru and the *True Sikh* and the perception of God Himself. The world according to Sikhism is not a mere appearance; it is definitely real. Even, with the attainment of the final beatitude, the world remains real. The Guru and the True Sikh perceive everywhere the grandeur of Brahman. God perceives His Creation and enjoys the sport (*lila*). The second source of knowledge *i.e.* inference is based on perceptual knowledge. It includes comparison and presumption as well. The third source of knowledge is *Sabda* or verbal testimony. The testimony may either be sacred or secular.

Adopting the above-mentioned three sources of knowledge, the Sikh Philosophy presents forth the following thoughts about Brahman, Jiva and Maya:

Brahman is One without a second. His Name is Truth. He is the Creator, devoid of fear and enmity. He is Immortal, Unborn and Self-existent. He is Truth, Consciousness and Bliss. He is Omnipresent, Omnipotent and Omniscient. He is Changeless and Flawless. When He wills to become many, He begins His Sport like a juggler. He creates the universe and brings the matter out of Himself. Before the creation, He is in abstract meditation (*Sunya Samadhi*) and qualityless (*Nirguna*), but after the creation, He, as *Ishvara*, manifests Himself as treasure-house of qualities (*Saguna*). He is faultless, good, holy, light, primal cause and essence, beyond our cognizance, pervasive and everlasting.

He is a *Purusha*, who creates the whole universe. There is none other separate eternal entity except God. He is the Creator of *Prakriti* and three *gunas* (qualities) *i.e. rajas, tamas* and *sattya*. He is a *Purusha* distinct from other *Purushas* (*jivas*). He is *Adi Purakh* (who is from the very beginning), *Sat Purakh* (pervasive and everlasting). *Karta Purakh* (Creator), *Akal Purakh* (uninfluenced by Time) and *Niranjan Purakh* (without the influence of *maya*).

Jiva is a miniature of Brahman. It should not be mistaken for Brahman Himself. It has its on individuality, but since it comes out of Brahman, it carries the qualities of Brahman. It is immortal. The physical body decays, but it continues for ever.

According to the *Adi Granth*, *Prakriti* or *maya* is not a separate ultimate reality. It has been created by God. It takes the individual away from God and thus leads him towards transmigration. When the influence of *maya* vanishes, the *jiva* realises Brahman. When Brahman comes into contact with *maya* of three *gunas* (qualities), the process of creation begins. The unconscious matter and the finite selves, which exist in Brahman before the creation, join this process by a gracious act of His Will.

The Sikh Gurus are of the view that it is wrong to delimit the Creation of the Lord. Whereas the Lord Himself is without limits, His Creation cannot be considered within limits. There are countless universes and in the them there are many species of diverse forms and colours. The *Pauranic* idea of eighty-four lakhs of species is found in the *Adi Granth*. There are lakhs and crores of upper and nether regions. "From God arose air, from air water, from water the three worlds, with His light in every self"—(Guru Nanak). The theory of creation propounded by the Sikh Gurus resembles *Brahmparinamavada* of Ramanuja, which presents forth the *Sankhyan* theory of evolution, but emphasises that *Prakriti* is absolutely dependent upon God. Guru Nanak says, "Nobody knows the exact time when the universe was created, except the Creator Himself."

The Truth (Brahman) is immanent in the universe. The human body is its repository. The body is not merely a thing like other objects, it is an epitome of the universe. It is a microcosm, whereas the universe is macrocosm. Therefore, whatever exists in the universe, also exists in the body of a human being. This implies that the same energy is in action, both in the human body and the vast cosmos, therefore, the seeker should not get himself lost in the vastness of the cosmos and only cocentrate himself on the Truth within his own body.

The Sikh Gurus opposed strongly all the distinctions of caste. They believed in universal brotherhood. According to them, the religious practices and other *Karmas* created ego and this ego could be overcome by the remembrance of the Name of the Lord and the grace of the True Guru. The ethical greatness was considered as a basis for spiritual greatness. The prominence was given to truth in life, but still greater prominence to the practice of truth. The active life of a householder was considered the best life and the division of society into *Varnas* and *Ashramas* was rejected. According to Sikh Philosophy, the ethical qualities leading towards the ideal of Spiritual Bliss are the real virtues. They can be put into practice by the people of all castes. With the practice and attainment of the attributes of God, the lowliest of lowly can become Godlike. The concept of God as Love and Grace has often been interpreted by the Western scholars as leading towards Passivism. But in the *Adi Granth*, we find no scope for Passivism. The hand and the mind must be in action for the loftier ideal.

God is Gracious. He preserves everybody, whom he gives life. An individual should have no worry on the physical plane. His efforts are of no avail. He should seek His Grace, which will put him on the path of good actions and inward purity. These efforts on the spiritual plane bring him happiness. Thus the doctrine of *Karma* and Grace are combined. The *Adi Granth*, though holds that the Will of God reigns supreme, it does not deny freedom to individual. The reality of the world forms the basis of Sikh ethics. Though the world is transient, its existence is real.

In the *Adi Granth*, we find, the close combination of ethics and theology. The ideal is the realisation of God, but for this purpose, the attainment of godly attributes and the purity of morals is necessary. The purity of conduct leads us out of the evil influences of ego and *Maya* and makes the mind pure.

When the mind becomes pure, God is realised. The Sikh Scripture lays great emphasis on the society of the 'good' *i.e.*, *Sadh Sangat*. Modesty, tolerance, patience, service, right speech, simplicity, conscientiousness, appreciativeness, truth, justice, friendliness, mercy *etc.* are some of the qualities to be imbibed by an individual. Besides personal ethics, there is State ethics, which lays emphasis on the relations of an individual and his family with the State. "The reign of that ruler is lasting who follows the democratic Ideals"—(Guru Nanak).

The main purpose of the life of an individual is the realisation of the Lord of all creation. This can only be done by the grace of the True Guru, who has full knowledge of Brahman. In the perception of the Guru, there is nothing except Brahman. He is a field of *Dharma*. His benevolence is equal for all. The Guru gives Word or Name to his disciple. By remembering this Name, the wall of illusion is removed. True Guru is an ocean of truth and knowledge. Since the Guru himself is the light of knowledge, his words are a light for the world. The first and the foremost duty of a disciple is the remembrance of the Name, which is the only holy *Karma*. By repeating the Name of the Lord, all the sins are washed away, all the wishes are fulfilled and the state of final beatitude is obtained, the fear of death or *Yama* melts away.

In order to rise higher on the spiritual planes, one must get himself attuned to the Will of God. The human being acts and desires for worldly pleasures, which end in misery. In fact, God has given us good amount of free-will under His Will and those who act according to the will of God, realise the state of Bliss. Others, who are worldly-wise, undergo births and deaths. The wisdom of an individual is of no use. Everything happens under the Will of God. The attainment of the nectar of Name is the ideal under the Will of God. The individual can act freely for the attainment of this ideal, therefore, great stress is laid on fortitude, which forms the basis of the grace of the Lord.

The *karmas* done under the influence of *maya* and ego are the cause of transmigration. Without the attainment of the Name of the Lord, the cycle of births and deaths continues. There are innumerable individual selves taking different physical forms. The words virtue and sin, heaven and hell came in usage after the creation of the world of three *gunas* (qualities). The virtuous go to heaven and the sinners to hell. The *Bhakta* of the Lord has no desire to go to heaven. He does not fear hell. The true disciple rises above virtue and sin, heaven and hell. He loves the Lord and surrenders himself completely. His ideal is the attainment of the lotus-feet of the Lord. The state of bliss and joy at the feet of the Lord is inexpressible. He always remembers the Name of the Lord and is attuned to Him. The body is humble without this attunement. It opens the difficult knot of mind and *maya*. This state of realisation is called *Sehj*. The company of saints and good people is essential for the attainment of this state.

In *Jupji*, the epitome of the *Adi Granth*, Guru Nanak has mentioned five stages of spiritual development. These stages have been named as *Dharma Khand* (The region of duty), *Gian Khand* (The region of knowledge), *Saram Khand* (the region of effort), *Karam Khand* (the region of Grace) and *Sach Khand* (the region of Truth). Through these regions, the seeker rises from the moral plane to the spiritual plane.

The Sikh Philosophy is not merely metaphysical speculation, but is based on the immediate data of experience. This experience is super-sensuous and transcendental. The philosophy and religion are intermingled. The religious philosophy of the Sikh Gurus is propounded through their songs of love and devotion, which are contained in the *Adi Granth*. This scripture was compiled by the fifth Guru (*i.e.* Guru Arjan) of the Sikhs in 1604. It contains the Word or the *bani* of the Guru. The *Word* is the Guru Himself, therefore, Guruship was bestowed on this holy book by the tenth and the last Sikh Guru. The constituents of *Guru Granth Sahib* were composed in different periods. Jaidev, the Bengali saint of the twelfth century, is the oldest composer included in this holy book. Namdev, the famous Maharashtrian poet, belonged to the fourteenth century. Kabir, the Hindi poet of the Gangetic valley flourished in the fifteenth century. Guru Nanak and his successors lived in the sixteenth and seventeenth centuries. Thus we find, that the Sikh scripture covers a span of six centuries. The selection of the *bani* was made on the basis of ideology.

The second Sikh scripture is *Dasam Granth*, which contains the religious and narrative poetry of the tenth Guru, who elucidated the philosophy of the *Adi Granth* in his religious verses. This Guru founded Khalsa and brought forward the 'Cult of the Sword.' He symbolised *Ishvara* as All-Steel and *Maha Kal*. The Sikh elucidator of **Gurmat Philosophy** was Bhai Gurdas, who lived from the time of Guru Amar Das to that of Guru Hargobind.

2

Sikh Philosophy

The Concept of Brahman

In Indian Philosophy, the ultimate reality is called Brahman. In Sikh scriptures, this word occurs very often. It is pronounced as Brahm. Guru Arjan, the compiler of the *Adi Granth*, has written the following words about Brahman:

Whatever I see, is Brahman,
Whatever I hear, is Brahman.[1]

In fact, the whole of the *Adi Granth* talks about Brahman and His Divine Will. The real motive of our birth in this world is the realisation of Brahman.

The real nature of this ultimate reality has been summed up in *Mul Mantra*, the fundamental sacred prayer. This sacred text contains the following words:

Ik-Aumkar Satnam Karta Purakh Nirbhau Nirvair Akal Murat Ajuni Saibhang Gurparsad.

The translation of this sacred text is:

God (Brahman) is One. His Name is Truth. He is the Creator. He is without any fear and enmity. He is Immortal, Unborn and Self-Existent. He can be realised through the Guru (Preceptor).

The first word of this sacred formula is significant. It is the first word of the *Adi Granth*. It is composed of *Ik* plus *Aumkar*. It means that *Aumkar* is One. The word *Aum* occurs in *Upanishads*. In *Kathopanishad, Yama* answers to Nachiketas in the following manner:

THE CONCEPT OF BRAHMAN

"That which all the Vedas declare, That which all austerities utter, That, desiring which they lead the life of *Brahmacharya*. That Word I tell thee briefly: It is *Aum*. That Word is even Brahman; that Word is even the Supreme."

The word *Aum* occurs also as *O-Am* and *O-Amkar* in the *Adi Granth*. Guru Nanak says in his longer poem *Dakhni O-Amkar*:

By O-Amkar Brahma was created.
By O-Amkar Chit (Consciousness) was created.
By O-Amkar Time and Space were created.
By O-Amkar Vedas were created.
The Word O-Amkar bestowed final emancipation on jivas.
By repeating O-Amkar the disciples obtained release.
Listen to the comments on the Syllable O-Am
The syllable O-Am is the essence of Three Worlds.[2]

The word *Aumkar* occurs in *Mandukyopanishad* and *Prashnopanishad*. In the very first *shloka* of *Mandukyo-upanishad* it is written:

Bhutam bhavad bhavishyad iti sarvam aumkar eva:
It is translated as: All that is past, present and future, all this is only the syllable *Aum*.

In the second *Shloka* of the fifth question of *Prashnopanishad*, the word Aumkar occurs thus:

Etad vai, Satyakama, param chapram cha brahma yad Aumkarah:

This verse means: "Verily, O Satyakama, this *Aumkar* is the Supreme and the Lower Brahman." And these terms 'Supreme Brahman' and 'Lower Brahman' are explained in *Brhadaranyakopanishad* in the following manner:

"There are two states of Brahman, formful and formless, changing and unchanging, finite and infinite, existent and beyond existence."

In *Mandukyo-upanishad* the syllable *Aum* has been split up in three parts A, U and M or *Akara*, *Ukara* and *Makara* Vaishvanara, whose sphere of activity in waking state is the letter A or *Akara*. *Taijasa*, whose sphere of activity is the dream state, is the letter U or *Ukara*. Prajna, whose sphere of activity is the state of deep sleep is the letter M or *Makara*. These three state of mind do not exist in *Turiya*, the fourth state or *Chautha Pad*. In *Turiya*, the *Jiva* and Brahman become one. Thus the word *Ik-Aumkar* in the *Adi Granth* may signify one Brahman, out of which evolves the world of three states.

A—Akara—Waking State
Ik-Turiya-Aumkar-U—Ukara—Dream State
M—Makara—Deep Sleep

On one side, there is unmanifested absolute and on the other the personal *Ishvara*. The personal *Ishvara* performs three functions of creating, preserving and destroying, therefore the word *Ik-Aumkar* may signify the unity of Brahman (both Supreme and Lower) out of which evolve three distinct powers named in Hindu Mythology as Brahma, Vishnu and Shiva.

Supreme Brahman) *Ik* (*Aumkar* Lower Brahman   Brahma (Creator)
Unmanifested   Manifested   Vishnu (Preserver)
                                              Shiva (Destroyer)

The scholars have given different interpretations of *Ik-Aumkar*:

1. It signifies that the *Ultimate Reality* is *One* (*Advaita*) conveying thereby that *Jiva* and *Ishvara* are one.
2. The figure One is suggestive of *One Name* common to all. The Vedas lay some restrictions regarding the Divine Teaching. But Guru Nanak broke all the barriers of caste. *Aumkar* is suggestive of the Vedic teaching, while the figure *one* is put to differentiate the Vedic and Non-Vedic teachings.
3. Etymologically, *Aum* is a derivative from the root *Ava*; which means to preserve and protect. Thus *Ik-Aumkar* means: The One, who protects.

The words *Brahm* and *Para Brahm* occur in the *Adi Granth* for Lower Brahman and Higher Brahman respectively. The Higher Brahman is devoid of attributes. He is indeterminate and incomprehensible. He is transcendental being called Truth. This Truth is without beginning and end. He is Consciousness and Bliss. He is non-phenomenal, non-spatial, non-temporal, non-causal, impersonal and devoid of all sensible qualities. He is '*Neti Neti*' and can be described by the method of negation. He is unborn, eternal, infinite and self-existent. He is flawless and taintless. He is also called *Nirguna Brahman* (without any qualities). Some quotations

from the *Adi Granth* regarding this aspect of Brahman are given below:
1. Thou art immortal Purusha, uninfluenced by time;
   Thou art non-temporal Purusha. inaccessible and unparalleled.[3]   *Maru*, M. 1.
2. Thou Higher Brahman, Supreme Ishvara.[4]
   Var Maru, M.V.
3. Indefinable, immeasurable, inaccessible, beyond the cognizance of the senses. He is uninfluenced by time and action.
   Undifferentiated, Unborn, Self-Existent, He is without fear and illusion.
   I surrender myself to All Truth.
   He is without form, colour, and delineation;
   He is realised through True Word.
   He hath no mother, no father, no son, no relation, no wife and no sexual instinct.
   Thou partless, taintless and transcendental Brahman, All the Light is Thine.[5]   *Sorath*, M. 1.

The Lower Brahman is also called *Sagun* Brahman and *Ishvara*. He is endowed with attributes. He is immanent in the phenomenal world. He is the Lord of the spatial and temporal world, governed by casuality. He is infinite, eternal, omnipresent, omnipotent and omniscient. He is the creator, preserver and destroyer of the Universe. He is the Lord of the law of *Karma* and is the inner controller. He is Truth, Consciousness and Bliss. He is the Higher Soul or Supreme Self (*Paramatma*).

The sacred formula (*Mul Mantra*) given above needs elucidation. *Ik-Aumkar* establishes the unity of Brahman. The Higher Brahman has no beginning and no end. He manifests Himself as Lower Brahman through Creation. Any one of His three main powers of Creation, Preservation and Destruction cannot be called Brahman. With the dissolution of the world, the Lower Brahman with these three powers is no more manifest. In Hindu thought, these powers are represented by Brahma, Vishnu and Shiva. The gods of this trinity lose their entity with the dissolution of the world. These gods are said to die, when Brahman dissolves. His Creation. On this basis, the Sikh scriptures have rejected the worship of gods and goddesses.

In its monotheism, the Sikh Faith resembles Islam and that is the reason why some historians have emphasised that Sikhism is the product of the impact of Islam on Hinduism. But a deeper study exhibits the differences in the conception of Godhead. God of Islam is Personal, but the saint-poets of the *Adi Granth* sing of an Impersonal God. Muslims believe that Muhammad is His prophet, but this prophethood of God has been rejected by the saints.

Brahman is one and without an equal or a lieutenant.[6] Zoroastrian theology divides Brahman into two parts viz. *Ahura Mazdah* and *Ahriman*. Christ proclaims himself as the son of God. But these views are not acceptable to the Sikh Gurus. Brahman is indivisible. He has no son, but He is the parent or father of all. *Adi Granth* recognises the fatherhood of God like Islam.

Besides emphasising the unity of Brahman, the Sikh Scripture talks of Lower Brahman as Perfect and preasurehouse of qualities (*Puran, Sampuran, Gun Tas, Guni Gahir, Gun Nidhan, Bemohtaj*), who is faultless and flawless (*Abhul, Adal, Achhal, Abhang, Achhed, Avgat, Amolak*), who is light (*Prakash, Jot*), who is Good and Holy (*Pavittar, Punit, Pavan, Pak*), who is beautiful (*Sunder, Suhan, Gauhar, Lal, Gulal, Ratnagar*), who is almighty (*Sarab shaktiman, Samarth, Asur, Sanghar Sabal Mallan, Balah Chhallan, Akal Kala, Bhuj Bal, Chatarbhuj*), who is omnipresent (*Ape Ap, Hadra Hadur, Sarab Biapi, Sarab Niwasi, Sarbatr Ramnang, Bharpur*), who is omniscient (*Janoi, Jananhar, Gian, Chit, Dana, Bina*), who is the primal cause and the essence (*Mul, Tat*), who is beyond our cognizance (*Asujh, Nirbujh, Gupt, Agadh, Agah, Agam, Akah, Beshumar, Apar, Amit, Bisiar, Apar Apara, Bekimat, Adrisht, Atol, Akaram, Akrai, Varnan Chihnan Bahra*) and above all, who is Truth, all-pervasive and everlasting (*Sach, Sachidanand, Sarbang Sacha*).

His name is Truth. He must be called *Sat* or Truth, because he is always Truth. All other names except *Satnam* are *Kirtam* (composed) names.[7] There are several *Kirtam* names used in the poetry of Sikh Gurus and other saints, because they were more clearly understood by the people of different sects. The Vaishnavas used the following names: *Bhagwan, Bishan, Gobind, Gopal, Gosain, Hari, Narayan, Madho, Raghurai, Ram, Krishan,*

THE CONCEPT OF BRAHMAN 21

Vasudeva, Prabhu, Banwari, Kavala Kant, Sri Pat, Bawan Rup, Brah, Gajpati, Narsingh, Machh, Katchh, Chattar Bhuj, Lakshmibar, Chakradhar, Murari etc. The Shaivas called God by the names of *Shiva, Ishavara, Rudra, Nil Kanth* etc. The Muslims named him as *Rabb, Allah, Razaq, Khuda* etc. The name to which the Sikhs attach special significance is *Wahiguru*, which has been used in their verses by the Bhatts (Bards). In the verses of the Sikh Gurus, this name does not occur in full. It is found split into two parts *i.e. Wahu* and *Guru*.

Brahman is the Creator or *Karta*. He is called *Kartar, Siranda, Khaliq, Sirjanhar, Karn Karan, Pran Data, Pran Pati, Swaranhar*. He is a *Purusha*, who creates the whole Universe. There is none other separate eternal entity except God. He is the Creator and thus the Master of the Universe (*Sahib, Malik*). He creates *Prakriti* of the three *gunas* (qualities). The finite selves or *Purushas* emanate from Him. Unlike other *Purushas* (*Jivas*), He is a *Purusha*, who is from the very beginning (*Adi Purakh*) and who is all-pervasive and everlasting (*Sat Purakh*), who is the Creator (*Karta Purakh*), who is uninfluenced by Time (*Akal Purakh*) and who is without the influence of *Maya* (*Niranjan Purakh*).

Before the Creation of the World, there was nothing except Higher Brahman (*Para Brahm*), who was absorbed in abstract meditation (*Sun Samadhi*).[8] The Universe came into being when it was His will.[9] Brahman is without fear and enmity. These are ethical qualities and attributes of Brahman. Any one, practises these qualities in life goes near God-realization. There are several moral attributes of God mentioned in the *Adi Granth*. Since God is without fear, He is always in the state of bliss (*Nihal, Prasann, Harakhwant, Rang, Anand, Binod, Sachidanand*). He has no worries (*Beparwah, Nehkantak*). Since God is without any enmity. He is always Just: Graceful and Benevolent (*Dukhlath, Sagal Sukh-Sagar, Sukhehgami, Sukhdai, Sukhdata, Amrit, Mithbolra, Nimribhoot, Sahai, Garib-Niwaz, Din Dard, Din Bandhap, Din Dayal, Anath Nath, Nithavian Thaon, Dial, Karim, Rahim, Meharban, Karnamai, Rabb, Dukhbhanjan, Adli, Paij Rakhanhar, Bird Palanhar, Bakhshind, Nistaranhar, Patit Pawan, Ola* etc). He is always full of love for his lovers and He is father, mother, husband, friend and everything for them (*Bhagat Vachhal, Pita,*

Mata, Kant, Bhatar, Khasam, Dulha, Bharta, Bhai, Mitr, Sangi, Sathi, Sajan, Sakha, Yar, Priya, Piara etc.)

Brahman is Timeless Being. Time or *Kal* has no influence on Him,[10] therefore, he is always the same (*Ik-ras, Ik-ves*). He is ever new and fresh (*Nit Nawan, Navtan*). Whereas he is formless (*Arup, Nirankar*) and colourless (*Arang*), as a Being, he is beautiful (*Sundar, Manmohan, Manoramang, Jagmohan, Sohna, Nadanot*), Playful (*Choji*), Ecstatic (*Wahu Wahu, Khub Khub, Ascharj*) and Sublime (*Ucho Ucha, Dur*). He does not come in the womb (*Ajuni*). This attribute of God voices the rejection of the *Avatara* theory. Brahman is self-existent. He is from the beginning (*Adi*), the very beginning (*Parmadi*) and even has no beginning (*Anadi*). He can only be realised by the Grace of the True Guru (*Gur Prasad*). The term Guru in the *Adi Granth* means the Divine Teacher. God Himself is described as *Adi Guru* and *Jugadi Guru* i.e. He is the Divine Teacher in the beginning and the Primal age.

Brahman pervades in his created Universe, which may be called his body. The Universe is within him and he is within the Universe. That is the reason of the identification of the Universe as Brahman. Guru Amar Das says:

This Universe that thou seest is the manifestation of Hari.[11]

Ramkali, Anand, M. III.

Guru Arjan perceives Brahman everywhere, as is evident from the quotation given in the beginning of this chapter.

Guru Gobind Singh, the tenth Guru of the Sikhs, in his poetry in *Dasam Granth* has portrayed the Omnipotent and Almighty Brahman as Supreme Spirit regarded as the Destroyer of the evil forces (*Maha Kal*) and 'All-Steel.' The armours of steel have been considered as the symbols of the Primal Power.

The Concept of Jiva

The word *Jiva* has been used for soul, the finite self or the finite being. Whereas *Brahman* is infinite. *Jiva* is finite. Both

THE CONCEPT OF *JIVA*

Brahman and *Jiva* are *Purushas* in the background of *Prakriti*, but whereas *Brahman* or Supreme *Purusha* is the Creator of *Prakriti* and does not come under its influence, *Jiva* or *Purusha* plunges into the field of action or *Prakriti* and repeatedly suffers births and deaths. In the words of *Mundakopanishad*, Brahman and *Jiva* are like the two birds sitting closely on the self-same tree. They are fast bound companions. One of them eats sweet fruit, while the other looks on without eating.

The relation of *Brahman* and *Jiva* has been expressed by Guru Arjan in the following manner:

He (Brahman) does not die I (*Jiva*) have no fear.
He does not perish, I have no worry.
He is not poor, I am not hungry.
He is without sorrow, I am without grief . . .
He has no ties, I am not bound.
He does not toil, I do not sweat.
He is not impure, I am not tainted.
He is Blissful, I am always ecstatic.
He has no worry, I have no anxiety.
He is uninfluenced, I am without any effect.
He is not hungry, I am not thirsty.
When He is Pure, then I am deemed holy . . . .
On meeting the Guru, the illusion has been removed,
He and I have become one, imbued with the same hue.[12]

Asa, M.V.

Jiva is a sort of miniature of *Brahman*.[13] It has its own individuality, but since it comes out of *Brahman*, it carries the qualities of Brahman.

Jiva, like Brahman is deathless.[14] Before the creation, it lives within Brahman and at the time of creation, it comes into the world and takes bodily forms according to the Will of Brahman. The physical body decays, but the *Jiva* or *Purusha* continues for ever. The following thoughts about the nature of *Jiva* are found in the *Adi Granth*:

Neither it is human being, nor a god,
Neither an ascetic practising restraint, nor a Shaivite,
Neither a Yogi, nor an ascetic renouncing all wordly
　　achievements.
Neither it has a mother nor it is a son.
Who lives within this temple?

No body knows its specifications.
Neither a householder, nor an *Udasi* (ascetic).
Neither a king, nor a beggar,
Neither it has a body, nor blood,
Neither a Brahman, nor a Kshatriya.
Neither an ascetic practising austerities, nor a Sheikh
   (Muslim Divine).
Neither it is alive nor it dies.
If any one weeps on its seeming death,
He loses the grace of his personality   *Gaund*, Kabir[15]

It is a strange story, quite strange,
The soul is like God Himself.
Neither it is old, nor young.
Neither it is prone to misery, nor it dies.
It never dies, but exists from the very beginning.
Neither heat nor cold hath any effect on it.
Neither it hath an enemy nor a friend.
It neither experiences joy nor sorrow.
It is the master of all—the doer,
It hath no father, no mother,
But continues to exist from the limitless times,
Virtue and sin have no effect on it.
It is always awake within every heart.[16]   *Gaund*, M.V.

The above description of the soul makes its nature quite clear. The soul like God is uninfluenced by any outer agency. It does not love any particular form of body. The body is sagnificant only because of the presence of this *Vairagi* (ascetic). Guru Arjan addresses the body in this way:

In his company thou hast individuality in all respects.
Without him thou art clay.
He is a *Vairagi*, who lives for ever
And acts under the Will of God.
God brings both together and separates them.
He knows His Nature Himself.[17]   *Asa*, M.V.

The body has been considered as the wife of *Purusha*. The wife requests her husband to remain with her for ever, but the husband works under the Will of its own master (God):

The wife with folded hands requests:
"Do not go away, my Lord! Live in my house,

Do such business within the house.
That the hunger and thirst may vanish away."
The Lord says, "I am under His (Brahman's) will,
"Who is great and favours none.
"I shall live with you according to his will,
"Whenever He calls, I shall go away."[18]   *Maru*, M.V. Solha

The *Jiva* gives consciousness to the body, which becomes the play-ground of the senses and sense-organs. The mind and intellect control the working of the senses. In *Kathopanishad* it is written:

"Know the soul as the rider of the chariot, intellect as the charioteer and mind as the reins. The senses are the horses and their objects are the roads. The enjoyer is endowed with body, sense and mind."

The rider of the body-chariot is the enjoyer. The sense-organs, are directed by the mind; the mind works under the direction of intellect (*buddhi*) and the intellect is directed by the finite self. Thus *Jiva* is the active agent. It knows through the intellect and enjoys through the senses and the mind. When the mind and intellect are impure and uncontrolled, the finite self enters into bondage and experiences births and deaths. It experiences joys and sorrows because of its actions. The actions are the result of desires.

The ancient sages have mentioned five sheaths in which the *Jiva* is encased. The uppermost sheath is the bodily sheath, which is sustained by food. It is called *annamya kosha*. The next sheath is the vital sheath, known as *pranamaya kosha*. It is sustained by vital forces. Then there is mental sheath called *manomaya kosha*. It constitutes the functions of the mind. The next sheath, which depends upon the functions of the intellect, is the intellectual sheath or *vijnanamaya kosha*. The last sheath, which is not merely a covering, but the very essence of the individual self, is the blissful sheath or *anandamaya kosha*. Unless the upper sheaths which constitute the activities of the senses, sense-organs, mind and intellect, drop down from above the soul, the blissful state cannot be realised. The blissful and ecstatic state is known as *Turiya*. For the realisation of this state, the finite self has to iser above the three (waking, dream and deep sleep) states.

The *Jiva* transmigrates from one body to the other in accordance with its merits and demerits. It cannot escape the fruit of its actions. In itself, it is unborn and eternal but when associated with sense-organs and mind, it enters the cycle of births and deaths. The physical body becomes lifeless, when *Jiva* leaves it. The relation of the body and *Jiva* has been portrayed in the following hymn:

In his (Jiva's) company thou wert playful.
In his company thou wert associated with others.
In his company thou wert sought by everybody,
Without him, none liked thy presence.
Where goes the *Vairagi* (ascetic)?
Without him; thou art miserable.
In his company thou art significant in the house,
In his company thou art known to the world,
In his company thou wert decorated,
Without him, thou art deserted.
In his company thou art respected and honoured,
In his company, thou art related to the world.[19]   *Asa*, **M.V.**

Jiva being part and parcel of Brahman, is itself Brahman, when Avidya or ignorance vanishes. When the egg of illusion bursts forth.

"Brahman is merged in Brahman, none can separate it."[20]

Suhi, **M.V.** *Chhant.*

The Concept of Maya

Maya has been defined in the *Adi Granth* as that power, which takes us away from Brahman.[21] *Jiva* forgets the Lord because of *Maya*. It is not a separate ultimate reality. It has been created by Brahman.[22] The word *Maya* is as old as *Rigveda*, but *Mayavada* came into existence with Shankara in the ninth century AD. Shankara's position is: "*Brahman Satyam Jagan Mithya Jivo Brahmaiva na'parah.*" "Brahman is the only reality; the world is an illusion or a false appearance; the individual soul is identical with Brahman." This principle of illusion is known as *Maya*. Through this illusion the self believes that it is an individual. This individuality

experiences plurality of the names and forms (*name-rupa*).
Adi Granth accepts this view that the illusion of *Maya* takes the individual away from God and thus leads him towards transmigration. When the influence of *Maya* vanishes, the *Jiva* realises the false appearance of the world.

The three *gunas* (qualities) are created through *Maya*. Brahman is said to have two forms—the first as Immanent in the world (*vikaravartin*) i.e. coming into contact with *Maya*, the second as transcendent (*trigunatita*) i.e. dissociating from *Maya*. The first form is known as *Saguna* and the second *Nirguna*.

He (Brahman) is *Nirguna* as well as *Saguna*,
Who hath illusioned others by wielding *Shakti*.[23]
Gauri Sukhmani.

The power of this *Maya-shakti* has been portrayed by Guru Arjan in the following hymn:

Who loves it (*Maya*) is devoured by it,
Whoever finds comfort in it, is greatly frightened by it,
Because of it, the brothers, friends and relatives quarrel with each other;
But with the grace of the Guru, I have subdued it.
They saw it thus and fell in love with it,
The adapts, *Siddhas*, gods and men,
Without the preceptor all were beguiled.
Some become stoics, but are sexually hungry,
Some collect it as householders, but cannot own it.
Some become famous as donors, but are much worried by it,
I surrendered myself at the feet of the Guru and was saved by Hari.
The devouts practising penance were misled by it,
The Pandits were subdued through all-conquering greed.
The three *gunas* (qualities) and heaven were misled by it.
I was saved by the grace of the Guru
It is subdued by the person with True knowledge.
It prays to him with folded hands:
"I shall do whatever you bid me."
But the true disciple does not come near it.[24]   *Asa*, M.V.

Guru Amar Das has put a question about *Maya*, but answered it in the same breath:

What is *Maya* and what is its function?
This *Jiva* is in bondage of happiness and misery and functions

in ego.[25]

Thus *Maya* is the bondage for *Jiva* and its main functionary is ego. The world of *Maya* is the world of three *gunas* (qualities). These three *gunas* are the resultants of ego or *Ahamkara*. These three *gunas* are named: *Tamas, Rajas* and *Sattva*. *Tamas* is resistance, *Rajas* is motion and *Sattva* is rhythm When these qualities are in equilibrium, there is inactivity and the *Maya* of the Lord is asleep. When it is the Will of the Lord, the state of inequilibrium of the qualities begins. The *Maya*, the consort of the Lord is awake and the three powers of the Lord *i.e.* Creation, Preservation and Destruction become manifest. Guru Nanak says in *Japji*.

> Brahman and *Maya* came into contact and *Maya* conceived.
> Three disciples were born from her.
> One is the creator, the other sustainer
> And the third destroyer.
> They work under the direction and orders of Brahman.
> He sees them, but they see him not: A wonder of wonders.[26]

The above verses make it clear that Brahman, Vishnu and Shiva are the children of *Maya*. They are the representatives of three *gunas* (qualities).

The above-mentioned description of *Maya* is its one aspect, which is in relation to Brahman. In this aspect, it is the power (*shakti*) of Brahman. But there is another aspect of *Maya*, which is quite different from that of *Kavala, Sri* or *Lakshmi*. In this aspect it is portrayed as a detestable and ignominious woman, sometimes portrayed as a serpent.

> There are signs of anger on her forehead and in her eyes.
> She speaks harshly with her chattering tongue.
> She is always hungry and thinks that her Lord is far away.
> Brahman has created such a woman,
> Who has devoured the whole world;
> I have been saved by the Guru, O my brother,
> She has created illusion and conquered the whole world,
> She has subdued Brahma, Vishnu and Shiva.[27]   *Asa*, M.V.
> None is stronger than this she-serpent,
> Which has beguiled Brahma, Vishnu and Shiva.[28] *Asa*, Kabir
> *Maya* is clinging to the world like a she-serpent,
> Whoever serves it, is devoured by it;

Some True Disciple subdues it like a snake-charmer.[29]
Var Gujri, M. III.

This is another aspect of *maya*, which is in relation to *Jiva*. The attachment with *Maya* leads *Jiva* towards transmigration. The cycle of births and deaths ceases only, when *Jiva* rises above the fold of *Maya*. Kabir says:

Whomsoever He keeps uninfluenced by *Maya*,
I am his servant, saith Kabir.[30] *Bhairo*, Kabir

The word *Maya* has been used for wealth also. This *Maya* is like counterfeit merchandise, which when put to test loses all its value. When it slips away, the body loses its brigthness. It is fickle, but it is very beautiful and lustrous that everybody is attracted towards it. It is a temporary phase and the honour gained through it is also temporary.[31]

The mother, father, son and loving brother, all have been misled by her into duality,
Some have more duality, some less, all of them die quarrelling,
I bow before my True Guru, who has shown me this play.
The whole world is burning in this secret fire, but the devotee is uninfluenced by *Maya*.[32] *Dhanasari*, M.V.

The colour of *Maya* fades away in no time like the shade of clouds. The kings accumulate *Maya* and rule in ego, but it never accompanies them after death.[33] A serviteur of *Maya* is sans eyes and sans ears.[34] In *Maya* there are five vices *i.e.* lust, anger, greed, attachment and ego. In *Maya* there is death.

The Sikh Gurus have rejected the *Samkhyan* doctrine that *Prakriti* is a separate eternal entity. According to them *Maya* is the nature of Lower Brahman. It is his *Shakti*. But in relation to *Jiva* it has been symbolised as poison, a noose or an intoxicant. It is the cause of *Avidya* (ignorance) in *Jiva*.

The Concept of Creation

In the *Mul Mantra* occurring in the beginning of *Japji* (a poem of Guru Nanak, which is considered an epitome of the

Adi Granth) and repeated hundreds of times in the *Adi Granth*, *One ever existent* is called Karta-Purakh—the *Purusha*, who is the Creator. He creates, whenever it is His Will. Similarly, He dissolves the created Universe, whenever it is His Will. Before the Creation, He was in abstract maditation—this state of His is known as *Sunn Samadhi*. The earliest description of this state is contained in the *Nasadiya Suktā* of *Rigveda*.

This hymn of Creation has thus been translated by Macdonell:

    Non-being then existed not nor being:
    There was no air, nor sky that is beyond it.
    What was concealed? Wherein? In whose protection?
    And was there deep unfathomable water?
    Death then existed not nor life immortal:
    Of neither night nor day was any token.
    By its inherent force the one breathed windless
    No other thing than that beyond existed.
    Darkness there was at first by darkness hidden;
    Without distinctive marks, this all was water.
    That, which becoming, by the void was covered.
    That one by force of that came into being.
    Desire entered the One in the beginning:
    It was the earliest seed, of thought the product.
    The sages searching in their hearts with wisdom,
    Found out the bond of being in non-being.
    Their ray extended light across the darkness:
    But was the one above or was it under?
    Creative force was there, and fertile power:
    Below was energy, above was impulse:
    Who knows for certain? Who shall here declare it?
    Whence was it born and whence came this creation?
    The gods were born after this world's creation:
    Then who can know from whence it has arisen?
    None knoweth whence creation has arisen:
    And whether he has or has not produced it:
    He who surveys it in the highest heaven,
    He only knows, haply he may know not.

This hymn of yore is very similar to the hymn of creation written by Guru Nanak in *Raga Maru*, wherein the Great Guru says:

    There was darkness for countless years,

There was neither earth nor sky; it was His Will
There was neither day nor night, neither sun nor moon,
He was in abstract meditation.
When it was His Will, He created the world,
The wide Universe was suspended without any mechanism.
He created Brahma, Vishnu and Shiva.
And the attachment of maya was increased.[35]

The same idea has been expressed in twenty-first canto (*Ashtapadi*) of *Sukhmani* composed by Guru Arjan *viz.*

When this physical world was not seen, whence arose vice and virtue?
When He was in abstract meditation, then who bore enmity and for whom?
When the form and colour of this world was not seen, then who bore happiness or sorrow?
When Brahman was all alone, then who was attached or illusioned?
This world is His own *Lila* (Sport), none else is its Creator, saith Nanak.
When He created this physical world, He expanded the Universe in three *Gunas*.
The story of vice and virtue began; some went to hell and some aspired for heaven.
The noose of *Maya*, ego, attachment, illusion, fear, happiness, sorrow, honour and disgrace were explained in several ways.
He has created this *Lila* and sees it Himself; when he finishes His *lila*, He is all about saith Nanak.[36]

We find that the Vedic hymn even expresses doubt about the creative activity of Brahman, but the Sikh Scripture is very positive about it. Nevertheless, it may be said, that the Sikh Gurus have followed the *Rigvedic* line. There have been speculations about the time when Brahman created this Universe. Guru Nanak has emphatically rejected this stand, because the created one cannot know the creator:

The Pandits could not know the time;
  it should have been mentioned in the Puranas,
The Qazis could not know the time;
  it should have been mentioned in the *Quran*.
The Yogi does not know the time, the lunar date,

the day, the month and the seasons.
The Creator who has created the world, knows it Himself.[37]

Japji

The *Puranic* division of *yugas* (ages) is frequently mentioned in the *Adi Granth*. The state of darkness before the creation is described to have lasted for thirty-six *yugas*:

'Hari was in abstract meditation in the darkness lasting thirty-six yugas.'[38]

This measurement of time is *Pauranic*. It was crystallised belief of the times.

II

When it was His Will, Brahman created the Universe. But what was the process of creation? Wherefrom came the unconscious matter and the finite spirits? Ramanuja, who accepts the Upanishadic account of creation literally, believes that the manifold world has been created by God out of Himself by a gracious act of His Will. The unconscious matter and the finite spirits existed in Him before the creation. Guru Arjan takes a similar view about the creation, when he says:

All the matter (unconscious matter and finite selves) is within One.
It is seen in many colours.[39]

Sukhmani

The finite selves are part and parcel of Brahman, therefore, they are immortal. As regards the unconscious matter or *Prakriti*, we are to trace its evolution. *Prakriti* or *Maya* has been created by Brahman. The *Samkhyan* doctrine about the separate and independent entities of *Purusha* and *Prakriti* has not been accepted by the *Adi Granth*. Kabir says:

This female serpent is created by Him.
What power or weakness it can show?[40]

Asa, Kabir

Guru Amar Das in his famous poem *Anand* has discribed Shiva and Shakti both as the creation of God:

The Creator has created Shiva and Shakti both:
And keeps them under His Cosmic Law?

Anand[41]

In this sense Shiva and Shakti are *Purusha* and *Prakriti*, which are created by God Himself.

III

The following words occur in Upanishads: *Saikshat Bhasayan, Prajayey*, which means (Brahman), He will may, I become many; may I bring." This doctrine of Many from ONE also is

contained in the verses of the *Adi Granth*. Guru Arjan says:
   He becomes countless from ONE, saith Nanak,
   And everything dissolves into ONE.   *Majh*, M.V.[42]

In this Upanishadic thought, the consciousness is taken into consideration. But in the Puranas, the matter takes the place of consciousness. In this case, the matter becomes many.

In the Puranas, a vast atom called Mahat—the great—is the seed of the universe. This is presided over by an intelligence called *Purusha*. This atom of *Mahat* is taken as the substratum of the universe. It is further split into three types of Ahamkaras *i.e.* active, rhythmic and passive. They are named as *Rajasic, Sattvic* and *Tamasic*. Out of *Rajasic Ahamkara* which is called *Taijasa*, arise the organs of sense and Manas as the eleventh. Out of the *Sattvic Ahamkara* which is called *Vaikarika*, arise the conscious units of being called Devas. Out of the *Tamasic Ahamkara*, which is called *Bhutadi* arise the elements. With the generation of these elements, the bodies are composed. Thus *Tamasic Ahamkara* results in the physical world.

When Guru Nanak met the Yogis of his day, they asked him the following question besides others:
   O Purusha, How the world comes into being?
   By what foible it is dissolved?[43]
The great Guru gave the following reply:
   O Purusha, the world comes into being in Ahamkara,
   It goes away with the forgetfulness of the Name of the Lord.[44]
                                                    Siddh Goshta

In this quotation, Guru Nanak referred to the above mentioned thought.

IV

The evolution of *Mahat* into *Ahamkara* and thence to elements is the evolution of *Prakriti* in the *Samkhyan* thought. Besides *Purusha* there are twenty-four principles. *Prakriti* gives birth to *Mahat i.e.* intelligence or *Buddhi*. From *Buddhi* evolves *Ahamkara*. Five sensory organs, five motor-organs, *Manas*, five *Tanmatras* and five *Mahabhutas* are further evolutes. The 25th is the *Purusha*, untouched by this evolution.

Prakriti is also known as *Pradhan*. *Mahat* and *Pradhan* have been used in the *Adi Granth*, the former in *Japji* and the latter in Sukhmani.[45] The source of Mahat is Prakriti which is composed of three *gunas* (qualities). According to the *Adi Granth*, this *Prakriti* of three gunas was created by the Higher Soul:

> He created a Shakti of three gunas,
> The great maya is His shadow.[45]
>
> *Gaund*, M.V.

These three gunas are *Rajas, Sattva* and *Tamas*. According to *Samkhya*. when these gunas lose their balance, the creation begins. The evolute of *Mahat i.e. Ahamkara* is related to these three gunas. We have seen above that from the *Tamasic Ahamkara*, the elements are created. At first the five subtle essences or *Tanmatras* arise from the *Tamasic Ahamkara*. These essences are *Sabda, Sparas, Rupa, Rasa* and *Gandha*, which are called sound, touch, form, taste and smell respectively. From these subtle essences arise the gross elements or *Mahabhutas* which are *Akash, Vayu, Agni, Apas* and *Prithvi*. They are called ether, air, fire, water, and earth respectively. These correspond with the five states viz. etherial, aerial, gaseous, liquid and solid.

Out of the five *Mahabhutas i.e. Akash, Vayu, Agni, Apas* and *Prithvi*, the first one produces the second, the second produces the third and so on. The *Upanishads* and *Puranas* expound the same thought *i.e.* "From *Akash* arose *Vayu*, from *Vayu Agni*, from *Agni, Apas* and from *Apas, Prithvi*." At the dissolution of the universe, the reverse process starts *i.e. Prithvi* merges into *Apas, Apas* into *Agni* and so on.

The above process of creation from one *Mahabhuta* to another is mentioned in the *Adi Granth* in one of the hymns of Guru Nanak:

> From God arose Air, from Air, water,
> From water the three worlds, with His light in every self.[46]
>
> *Sri Raga*, M. 1.

All the *mahabhutas* could not be mentioned in one couplet. The first *mahabhuta* is *Akash*, whose subtle essence is *Sabda*. The first elemental creation was from *Sabda*. Guru Amar Das says in one of his hymns in *Raga Majh*:

> The creation and dissolution are through *Sabda*
> After dissolution, there is creation again through *Sabda*.[47]
>
> *Majh*, M. III.

Sabda and the Name are one. That is why Guru Arjan says in *Sukhmani*:

> All the creatures abide by Name.

The universe abides by Name.[48] *Sukhmani Canto*, No. 16.
Guru Nanak says in *Japji*:
He created the World with one WORD,
Lakhs of streams of life began.[49]   *Japji*.

Some people have argued that this thought of Guru Nanak is semitic in origin, but when we study carefully the *Nasadiya Sukta* of *Rigveda*, we find that Guru Nanak follows the *Rigvedic* line. His thought is found clearly in Samkhya and Puranas.

The idea of the creation from *mahabhutas* is found in several verses of the *Adi Granth*. In the concluding verses of *Japji*, we find the following thought about the *mahabhutas*:

Vayu, the preceptor; Apas, the father; Prithivi, the
                                                    mother; Mahat;
Day and night, the male and female nurses, make the world
                                                          play.[50]

VI

The idea of Hindu Trinity or *Trimurti* occurs several times in the *Adi Granth*. This concept of *Trimurti* is Pauranic. The three gods of *Trimurti* are Brahma, Vishnu and Shiva. These gods represent the three main powers of Brahman *viz.* the power of creating, the power of preserving and the power of destroying. Guru Nanak refers to these three attributes of Brahman in *Japji*.

The Lord married maya and three sons were born:
The one was the creator of the world (*i.e.* Brahma)
The one was the store-keeper and distributor (*i.e.* Vishnu)
The one was the holder of the court (*i.e.* Shiva)
But it is a matter of great wonder that He sees them,
And they cannot see Him.[51]

Being sons of maya, the gods of *Trimurti* cannot see or know Him *i.e.* Brahman. They represent three *gunas* (qualities). But the Hindus adored each one of them as Brahman. This henotheistic attitude (of Hindus) was not acceptable to Guru Nanak. Guru Nanak depicted only Brahman as omnipresent and omnipotent. Brahma, Vishnu and Shiva act according to His orders. Neither there is only one Brahma, nor only one Vishnu, nor only one Shiva:

There are many Vishnus and Shivas.
There are many Brahmas creating worlds of many forms and
    colours.[52]   *Japji*.

In fact, Brahman is the creator and Brahma is His creative attribute.

VII

There have been speculations about the extent of the Universe. Ptolemy believed in one thing and Copernicus in another. Christianity and Islam talk of fourteen regions, seven upper and seven nether. In his nocturnal journey in the company of Gabriel (archangel) and riding of Al-Boraq, the Holy Prophet is said to have crossed the six upper regions and entered the seventh to meet the Lord. Hinduism believes in fourteen Lokas or planes, the seven upper (*Bhurloka, Bhuvarloka, Swarloka, Maharloka, Janaloka, Tapaloka, Satyaloka* (or *Brahmaloka*), and the seven nether (*Atala, Vitala, Nitala, Gabhastimat, Mahatala, Sutala* and *Patala*). Sometimes it talks of three regions known as *Triloki* viz. Heaven, Earth and the Nether-world. The earth has been further divided into nine regions as *Nav-Khand*.

In the *Adi Granth*, there is mention of *Nav-Khand, Triloki* and *Chaudeh Bhavan*. The word *Khani* also occurs therein. A *Khani* is a division of creation. There are four major divisions of creation viz., *Jarayuja* (viviparous), *Andaja* (Oviparous), *Udbhija* (germinating) and *Svedaja* (generated by heat and moisture). This is the division of organic production. The inorganic production is called *jada*. The above-mentioned terms which occur in the *Adi Granth* are only illustrative terms and not those of a belief.

Guru Nanak talks of lakhs of upper and nether regions:
There are lakhs of nether and upper regions.[53] *Japji.*
Guru Arjan speaks of crores of upper regions:
There are crores of divisions of organic production.
There are crores of regions.
There are crores of upper regions and universes.[54]
Sukhmani.

Through their verses, both the Gurus say the same thing *i.e.* it is wrong to delimit the creation of the Lord. Whereas the Lord Himself is without any limits, His creation cannot be considered within limits. The Great Guru says;

There is no end to the physical world,
There is no end to His Creation.[55] *Japji.*

When Guru Nanak talks of the region of Piety in *Japji*, he talks only of our Earth, but on entering the region of knowledge, we find countless universes:

> There are many divisions of production,
> There are many divisions of speech,
> There are many kings.
> There are many contemplations,
> There are many servants,
> There is no end of it, saith Nanak.[56]   *Japji.*
> In the region of Truth, we find:
> There are regions, spheres and universes,
> If one describes, there is no end of them.[57]   *Japji.*

Even in our own universe, we find countless species of diverse forms and colours.[58] The *Pauranic* idea of eighty-four lakhs of species is found in the *Adi Granth*. Namdev, one of the saint-poets of the *Adi Granth* believes that half of these species live in water and the other half on Earth.[59]

VIII

The three principal Indian theories of creation are *Arambhvada*, *Parinamvada*, and *Vivartavada*. The first theory *i.e. Arambhvada* has been put forth by *Nyaya* and *Vaishesika Shastras*. It is also known as *Asatkaryavada* which signifies that the effect does not pre-exist in its cause. The effect is quite a new beginning. It is quite a fresh creation. According to this theory all physical things are produced by the combination of atoms. The saint-poets of the *Adi Granth* have not said anything in connection with this theory of creation.

The second theory of creation *i.e. Parinamavada* belongs to *Samkhya* and *Yoga Shastras*. It is also known as *Satkaryavada*. According to this theory, all the material effects are the modification of *Prakriti*. They pre-exist within the eternal *Prakriti* and at the time of creation come out of it and at the time of dissolution, they return to it. *Adi Granth* rejects the eternality of *Prakriti*. Only Brahman has been recognised as eternal, omnipresent and omnipotent; otherwise *Prakriti* and its evolutes have been accepted in the *Adi Granth*, as we have seen above.

The third theory of Creation *i.e. Vivartavada* has been put forward by Shankaracharya. According to this theory, the world is only a phenomenal appearance of Brahman. It is neither a real creation by Brahman nor a real modification of Brahman. The world only appears to us due to ignorance

(*Avidya*) and this creation is real only as long as *Avidya* lasts. But Ramanuja, another exponent of Vedanta after Shankaracharya, holds that the creation is relatively real. The world and the selves are as real as Brahman Himself. His theory is known as *Brahmaparinamavada*, because according to his theory the whole universe including the material world and the individual selves is a real modification of Brahman. God neither creates the matter and soul nor destroys them. The law of karma necessitates creation. But the Will of God is supreme. The creation and the dissolution of the world are His Lila or sport. Ramanuja believes in *Prakriti* like Samkhya, but according to him, it is absolutely dependent on God. It is controlled by God from within just as body is controlled by soul from within. *Adi Granth* like Ramanuja holds that the world is real. In the words of Guru Nanak:

The regions, universes, Lokas and physical formations are all real. *Asa di Var.*[60]

The theory of creation of the *Adi Granth* is very close to *Brahmaparinamavada*. The Macrocosm is reflected in Microcosm and one proclaims in wonder: Wahu! Wahu!! Wahu!!!

Microcosmic Theory as Enunciated in the Adi Granth

A hymn of Saint Peepa in the *Adi Granth* mentions both the macrocosm and microcosm.

God is in the body; the body is the temple of God,
In the body there are pilgrims and travellers;
In the body there are incense, lamps and the sacrificial food;
In the body there are the offerings of leaves.
After searching many regions, I have found nine treasures in the body.
Nothing is born and nothing dies. I say in the name of God,
Whatever is found in the Universe is found in the body;
Whoever searches it, shall find it.
Peepa says: God is the Primal Essence; He will be known

MICROCOSMIC THEORY IN THE *ADI GRANTH*

through the True Guru[61]   *Raga Dhanasari.*

The last two verses of the hymn given above are significant regarding our subject. Whatever is in the Universe is found in the body. The Universe is the *macrocosm* and the body is the microcosm. The soul lives in the body and the Higher Soul lives in the Universe. Since the soul and the Higher Soul are the same in Essence and the Higher Soul is reflected in the soul, similarly the universe is found in the body. A short treatise on the subject forms part of *Pran Sangali*, which is believed to be a part of the Apocryphal Literature in the name of Guru Nanak. This treatise begins with a reference to two hymns of the *Adi Granth*—one by Saint Peepa given above and the other is composed by Saint Beni. The translation of this hymn is given below:

Ira, Pingla and *Sukhmana* reside at one place;
There is Triveni at Prayag and let the mind take a bath there
O Saints: There resides the Pure Lord,
A few comprehend this, when they go to the Guru;
There at the confluence, the Pure One resides,
What are the signs of the abode of God?
There is played the unbeaten music of the Word,
There is neither sun nor moon, neither wind nor water,
Only he knows it, who follows the instructions of the Guru,
The Divine knowledge is produced and the evil departs,
The ambrosia trickles down.
Whoever knows this secret,
Shall meet the Primal Guru.
The tenth Gate is the abode of the inaccessible
There is a small chamber over the above, which contains the Treasure,
He, who keeps a watch over this, shall never fall asleep;
The three qualities and the three worlds shall not be in his contemplation.
He remains within the heart with the Name of the Lord.
He turns back his mind and fixes it on the Absolute.
He shall be wakeful and not utter a lie
And shall keep the five sense-organs under control,
He will treasure the instruction of the Guru in his heart.
And devote his mind and body to the love of God.
Within the Tenth Gate, there is light of a four-faced lamp.

There are endless petals of the lotus and the source is in the
   middle.
God dwells there with all His power.
Let man string the precious jewel of God's Name within him.
In the centre resides the Lord of the Three Worlds.
The five types of Musical Instruments are clearly heard;
Chauris appear to wave and shells to reverberate like thunder,
The pious by divine knowledge trample on their evil passions;
Beni begs for your Name.[62]   *Raga Ramkali*.

In both these hymns, there is mention of the secret recesses in the body. The hymn of Beni contains Yogic terminology. In fact, in the times of the Sikh Gurus, there were several types of Yogis in the country. The followers of Gorakhnath *i.e.* Naths were very strong in the Punjab. These Naths believed that the *microcosm* is a reflex of the macrocosm and that all the things that are found in the universe have their parallel in the body. Regarding this doctrine, the Nath cult resembled *Sahajayana* and *Kalchakrayana*.

The treatise mentioned above contains a conversation between the soul and the Higher Soul about the similarities in the body and the universe. *e.g.*
Then the soul said, "There are sun and moon in the universe.
   Where are they in the body?"
The Higher Soul replied, "These are eyes."
The soul said, "In the universe, sometimes there is light
   and sometimes there is darkness."
The Higher soul said, "When there is sleep, there is darkness
   and when one awakes, there is light.". . .
The soul said, "In the world, there are sixty-eight holy
   places of pilgrimage. Where are they in the body?"
The Higher Soul replied, "The good actions are like sixty-
   eight holy places of pilgrimage."
The soul said, "In the universe, there are heaven and hell.
Where are they in the body?"
The Higher Soul replied, "Whenever there is grief, it is hell
   and whenever there is comfort, it is heaven."[63]

The *Tantras* emphasised the significance of the body. The Truth is to be realised in and through the body. This was their cardinal belief and the whole of *Tantric Sadhana* was based on this belief. The body of man was considered the

MICROCOSMIC THEORY IN THE *ADI GRANTH*

residence of *Truth* and Truth could only be attained through the medium of the body.

The belief of the *Tantrikas* may be expounded further. The *Truth* is immanent in the universe. The human body is its repository. The body is merely a thing like other objects. It is an epitome of the universe, it is *microcosm*, whereas the universe is *macrocosm*. Therefore, whatever exists in the universe, also exists in the body of a human being. The physical processes of the universe and the biological processes in the human body are quite parallel. With this parallelism in view, the sun, moon, stars, mountains, rivers, islands etc. of the universe are located within the human body. This implies that the same energy is in action, both in the human and the vast cosmos, therefore, the *Sadhaka* should not get himself lost in the vastness of the cosmos and only concentrate himself on the *Truth* within his own body.

The saint-poets of the *Adi Granth* accepted the above mentioned Tantric doctrine in their own way. The path adopted by them for the realisation of the inner Truth was different from that of Nath Yogis. Some quotations from the *bani* of Guru Amar Das are given below:

There are innumerable things in this body;
The Pious after finding Truth, see them.
The release is obtained by entering the Tenth
   Gate and by passing the other nine gates, the unbeaten
   Music of the Word resounds.[64]   *Majh*, M. III.
There is vastness in this body.
The Name of the Pure One is inaccessible.
The Pious attains it.
One meets Him through His Grace.[65]   *Majh*, M. III.
Everything is there in the body, the regions, the spheres and
   the nether-worlds.
There are jewels in the body, there are stores of Bhakti.
There is the universe of nine regions within the body,
There are shops, bazars and cities.
The Name (full of nine treasures) is found in the body
   after contemplation on the Word of the Guru . . .
There are Fear and Love in the body, which are obtained
   by the grace of the Guru; . . .
Brahma, Vishnu and Shiva reside in the body.[66] *Suhi*, M. III.

None hath been able to evaluate this body,
My Lord hath created it.
The Pious control the body and meet the Lord.[67]

Maru, M. III.

The Concepts of Karma and Transmigration

Karma means action. Every *Jiva* desires, thinks and acts. Every action has its associations in the past, present and future. Every action is like a seed sown in the body, which is a field of action.[68] The soul (*Purusha*) is the farmer. It has been given a field in the form of a body. When the seed of action is sown, the consequences must follow. A *Jiva* repeatedly experiences birth in this world. The theory of *Karma* can be explained as the moral law of causation.

There are two types of *Karmas i.e.* Higher *Karmas* and Lower *Karmas*. The Lower *Karmas* (*i.e. Karam Kanda*) have been rejected by the Sikh Gurus. They have laid emphasis only on those *Karmas*, which lead us to the realisation of Brahman. From ethical point of view, the *Karmas* may be good or bad, virtuous or sinful. The remuneration of these *Karmas* depend on their quality. Whatever one did in his previous births, that makes his present life. Whatever the seed of actions is sown in the body, the harvest is reaped accordingly. As one sows, so shall he reap.[69] It is futile to slander others for the actions done. The fault lies in one's own actions.[70] Good actions not only bring the appreciation in this world, but also in the presence of the Lord.[71] Bad actions lead towards misery.[72] Bad actions are like a field of poison.[73] A bad person is like a thief. He is punished by the god of justice.[74] The slander of good people and the worship of the followers of mammon are considered as bad actions.[75] One should do such actions by which he may not feel ashamed in the presence of the Lord.[76]

These *Karmas* are done according to the Will of God. God has destined us from the very beginning for certain *Karmas*. We cannot escape them.[77] At this point a question arises, why should one be rewarded or punished, when one is not responsible for the actions? But a closer consideration of this line of thought brings us to the conclusion that saint-poets of the *Adi Granth* could not detach the *Karma* doctrine from God as was done by Jaimini, the author of *Purva Mimansa*. Kabir says:

This *Jiva* is tied by *Karmas*, you say,
But who gave life to *Karmas*? *Gaund*, Kabir.[78]

It is Brahman, who controls our *Karmas*. This does not mean that we ought to remain passive, because we have been denied even an iota of free-will. In order to rise higher on the spiritual planes, one must get himself attuned to the Will of God.[79] The human being desires, thinks and acts for worldly pleasures, which end in misery.[80] In fact, God has given us good amount of free-will under His Will and those who act according to the Will of God, realise the state of bliss. Others who are worldly-wise undergo births and deaths. The wisdom of an individual is of no use.[81] Everything happens under the Will of God. The attainment of the nectar of Name is the real ideal under the Will of God.[82] The individual can act freely for the attainment of the ideal, therefore, great stress is laid on fortitude, which forms the basis of the Grace of the Lord.

The *Karmas* done under the influence of *maya* and ego are the cause of transmigration. Without the attainment of the Name of the Lord, the cycle of births and deaths continues. There are innumerable individual selves taking different *physical* forms. The words virtue (*punya*) and sin (*pap*) and heaven and hell come in usage after the creation of the world of three *gunas* (qualities).[83]

The virtuous go to heaven and the sinners to hell. The true disciple has no desire of going to heaven. He does not fear hell.[84] He is above virtue and sin, therefore, he is above heaven and hell. Kabir says:

Which is the hell and which is poor heaven?
The saints condemn both.
We have nothing to do with any by the Grace of our Guru.[85]
Ramkali, Kabir

The saint, who is above heaven and hell, wishes to remain at the feet of the Lord for all times.[86]

Thus we see that heaven is not an ideal for a Sikh. The picture of hell has been depicted in the following manner:

There is a stream of fire from which emerge poisonous

flames.
There is none else there except the self.
The waves of the ocean of fire are aflame.
And the sinners are being burnt in them.[87] *Maru*, M. 1.

All the physical forms, through which the soul passes, are hells. Thus there are eighty-four lakhs of hells, there the sinners get due punishment for their deeds. The angels of death take away the sinner before the god of justice, who is depicted as money-lender (*Bania*). The scribes, Chitra and Gupta, are asked to give an account of the virtuous and sinful acts respectively. Then the god of Justice sends the sinners to hell. Before reaching the god of Justice, the sinner has to pay a toll tax in the way. This description of hell, god of Justice, Chitra Gupta etc. is Pauranic, through which the saint-poets of the *Adi Granth* wanted to create the hatred in the minds of the individuals against bad deeds and inculcate in them the devotion of the Lord, making it quite clear, that even good works could not get the release of the individual self.

The theories of *Karma* and transmigration are interlinked. All the orthodox and heterodox Indian Religions except Lokayatas (*Charvakas*) believed in these doctrines. The old Egyptians and Greeks also accepted them. The modern Theosophists have full faith in them. Some people believe that the soul existing from the very beginning takes birth in the world only once. This is the doctrine of pre-existence. Others are of the view that the soul takes birth repeatedly, but is only born as a human being and is never born as a bird or beast. This is the doctrine of re-incarnation. But according to the doctrine of transmigration, the soul takes various physical forms according to its *karmas*. The Indian sages talk of eighty-four lakhs of physical forms. Half of them live in water and the other half on land. In one of his hymns, Guru Arjan has described the various births of a soul:

The *Jiva* was born several times as worm and flying insect,
It was born several times as an elephant, a fish and a deer,
It was born several times as a bird and a snake,
It was born several times as a horse and a yoked bull,
Meet the Lord, this is the opportune time,
After a very long time, you have come in this body.
It was born several times as a stone and a mountain,

THE CONCEPTS OF KARMA AND TRANSMIGRATION

It was born several times as germs,
It was born several times as plants,
It strayed into eighty-four lakhs of physical forms.[88]

Gauri, M. V.

Jiva experiences bondage, when it enters the field of actions Every action enchains him further.[89] It tightens the noose round his neck.[90] There are three kinds of *Karmas*, *Sanchit*, *Prarabdha* and *Agami*. The *Karma*, which is ripe for reaping is called *Prarabdha*. The accumulated *Karma* of the past is *Sanchit* and the *Karma*, which is being created now is *Agami*. The *Prarabdha Karma*, cannot be avoided. *Sanchit Karma* manifests itself in the form of character. The chain of births and deaths ceases only on the exhaustion of *Prarabdha Karma*. The tie that binds *Jiva* to the wheel of births and deaths is desire.[91] In *Brhadaranyaka-upanishad* it is written, "When all the desires concealed in the heart, come to an end, the mortal becomes immortal and enjoys Brahman here."

Transmigration ceases with the exhaustion of desire. But the desire or *Trishna* comes to an end, when we meet the Knower of Brahman (*Brahm-Giani*) and act according to his instructions:

The fear of births and deaths ceases with the perfect
knowledge imparted by the Perfect Man.
We stray no more, our wanderings cease, on listening the
praises of the Lord, saith Nanak.[92]

Sukhmani

Trilochan, the Maharashtrian saint has said that the final desire at the time of death becomes a basis for our next birth. Whosoever remembers his sons at the time of death, becomes a pig. The person, who thinks of his houses becomes a ghost. The one who thinks of wealth becomes a snake. Whosoever remembers a woman, becomes a harlot.[93] This shows that a man may become a beast, a crawling snake or a woman in his next birth according to his *Karmas*.

The Concept of Hukm

Hukm is an Arabic word which means Order or Judgement of

God, prophet, ruler or a judge. In *Quran* pertains to the
Order of Judgement of God. In Muslim Theology it includes
the Order of Prophet as well. With the advent of Muslims, the
word was adopted in our language. Guru Nanak has defined
Hukm in a stanza of *Japji*:

By (Thy) *Hukm* the world of matter came into existence
(Thy) *Hukm* is inexpressible
By (Thy) *Hukm* the Jivas are created
By (Thy) *Hukm* they get distinction
By (Thy) *Hukm* they are good or mean
By (Thy) *Hukm* their destiny of joys and sorrows is scribed
By (Thy) *Hukm* some get thy benefaction,
By (Thy) *Hukm* some always lead life of misery.
Every body is within (Thy) *Hukm*
There is none outside it.
Whosoever realises the significance of This *Hukm*
He never talks in ego.[94]

The above verses give us a glimpse of the *Hukm* of God.
This *Hukm* is an over-all Order of the Lord. This Order is a
set of commandments or a set of the Laws of God. These laws
are true for all times and work in all the three fields *i.e.*
physical, moral and spiritual. All the creatures in the world
are bound by these laws.

The order of Judgement of a worldly ruler can be unjust,
but the *Hukm* of God is always just:

Mere words cannot bring justice,
He who takes poison, dies instantly
O Brother, see the truth and justice of the Creator,
Whatever one sows, he shall reap accordingly.[95]

Var Gauri, 1. M. IV.

Hukm may be identified with *Bhana* or the Divine Will. His
Will is His Order or His Judgement. Some people may declare
His will as unlawful because of ignorance. But the true working
of the laws of God is known only to those persons, who have
attuned their will to the Will of God. They never complain,
knowing fully well that He is always Just. If we are subjected
to several kinds of reverses in life, they are the result of our
own actions and are not the resultant of sudden anger of the
Lord. It is a fact that the Lord is All-Powerful. He may
destroy the creation in a moment. But the wise know this

destruction is always the result of some human failings. The law of cause and effect works in every field. The sorrows and griefs become a blessing in disguise and the worldly pleasures result in misery. The God-intoxicated persons know that:
   Several people experience sorrows, hunger and torture
   But this is all Thy gift.[96]

When it is the Will of the Lord, the world is created. It dissolves also according to His Will. But the law of cause and effect works throughout. Thomas Hardy, the famous English writer has brought out his thesis in his *Dynasts* that the world was created by the Lord in a semi-conscious state. That is the reason why there are sorrowful scenes in this world. The forces that work in the world are blind. But the Sikh Gurus talk of God as a 'thinking principle' and a conscious power:

   1. He sees, thinks and enjoys.[97]   *Japji*.
   2. He acts consciously (all alone by Himself).[98]   *Asa di Var*.

The God-intoxicated persons subdue their will to His Will, They accept, whatever befalls them during lifetime:
   Whatever the Lord does, is liked by the devotees.[99]
                                     Gauri, M. V.

The devotee is always happy under all circumstances:
   He who accepts the will of the Lord is always happy.
   He merges in Truth, Saith Nanak.[100]   *Asa*, M. III.
   Whatever was Thy Will, I experienced accordingly,
   Some rare person came under Thy Divine Will.
   Whosoever accepts Thy Divine Will feels comfort
   The Comfort is obtained only in Thy Divine Will.
   The *Manmukh* is blind and worldly-wise
   He does not accept the Divine Will and comes to grief
   He wanders in illusion and undergoes transmigration.
   He never attains the real refuge.[101]   *Maru Sothe*, M. III.

A few quotations depicting the *Hukm* of the Lord are given below:
   Through His *Hukm* He creates and dissociates
   Through His *Hukm* everything is created and also dissolved.
   Through His *Hukm* He becomes high-up and also lowly
   Through His *Hukm* He manifests Himself in several ways.[102]
                                Gauri Sukhmani, M. V.

Jiva was conceived with His *Hukm*, O dear! it came into the

womb.
It was born with His *Hukm*, O dear! with its head downwards
It came with his *Hukm*, O dear! and goes with His *Hukm*.
The evil-doer is tied up with His *Hukm*, O dear! and punished
The Word is recognised with His *Hukm*, O dear! and it goes
   in His presence
It falls into accounts with His *Hukm*, O dear! and is seized
   by ego and duality.
It experiences births and deaths with his *Hukm*, O dear! the
   evil doer weeps.
If this *Hukm* of the Lord is recognised, O dear! the *Jiva*
   realises truth and receives respect.[103]   *Sorath*, M. 1.
Gurmukh recognises the *Hukm* accepts it and merges in the
   Lord.
One comes in the world through *Hukm*
One merges in the Lord through *Hukm*
All the created world works under *Hukm*
The heavens, the seas, the nether-world are under His *Hukm*
His power works under His *Hukm*.
The earth and the bull bearing it are under His *Hukm*.
The wind, water and the sky are under His *Hukm*.
The *Jiva* resides in the house of Shakti under His *Hukm*.
The sport of the world is under His *Hukm*.
The wide expanse of the sky is under His *Hukm*.
The seas, plains, all the three worlds are under His *Hukm*.
All our breaths are under His *Hukm*.
And He sees everything under His *Hukm*.
He created the ten incarnations under His *Hukm*.
   and also countless gods and demons.
He who accepts the *Hukm* goes in His presence and merges in
   the true Lord.[104]   *Maru*, M. 1.
This is the sign of meeting the Lord:
— the recognition of True *Hukm* in the mind.[105]
                                                          Majh, M.V.

   All is Thy Nature, Thou art the Creator, the Pure OM
   He sees everything under his *Hukm* and acts
      consciously, saith Nanak.[106]   *Var Asa*, M. 1.
   The One Name is His *Hukm*.[107]   *Sri Raga*, M. 1.

The Concept of Grace

In Sikh Thought great emphasis is laid on the grace of the Lord. *Jiva* takes its birth in the world on account of *Karmas*, but the final liberation is attained only through the grace of God:

> The body takes its birth because of *Karmas*.
> But the salvation is attained through the Grace (of the Lord.)[108] *Japji*

But the question arises, if our *Karmas* do not bear the desired fruit of salvation, then why the Sikh Gurus have emphasised the importance of good actions. In a sense, the idea of Grace is antagonistic to *Karmas*.

The Gurus say:

1. This cup of love belongs to the Lord
   And whomsoever the Lord wants, He gives this cup to him.[109]   *Ramkali Var*, III.
2. My Lord is One, there is none other,
   He is realised by His Grace.[110]   *Asa*, M. 1.
3. With Thy Grace One attains the Highest state of bliss and narrates the indescribable story.
   Thou art the Creator, everything is Thy Creation, what is in the power of a *Jiva*?[111]   *Asa*, M. III.

The above quotations give an impression of the futility of human endeavour and the partiality and injustice of God. But that is not so. The Grace of the Lord begins with our acceptance of the true Path in life. The amount of Grace necessitates our accomplishments on the right path. In fact, the grace is not the result of any whim of the Lord, it begins and matures with beginning and maturity of our *dharma*. From the beginning of the grace upto the final emancipation, one works within the fold of grace.

1. Whosoever comes within His Grace, in him is born the faith and love following the path of truth and contentment, the pure mind is engrossed with the Word.[112]
   Asa, M. III.
2. Whosoever falls within His grace meets the Guru.[113]
   Asa di Var, M. I,
3. Through His Grace we serve the Guru

Through His Grace we serve (humanity).
Through His Grace this mind can be controlled
Through His Grace the mind becomes pure.[114]
Vadhana, M. III.
4. Truth is always Pure, the Truthful are also pure
Whosoever comes within His Grace, O Brother! attains
truthfulness. *Sorath*, M.V.[115]
5. Through His Grace this attachment ceases.
And one merges in the Lord. Saith Nanak.[116] *Asa*, M. 1.

This Grace is, in fact, the focussing of the special attention of the Lord on us, though otherwise we always remain within His sight.[117] We come under His special attention only when we turn our face towards Him and travel towards Him under His Light. Our ego vanishes.[118] Not only we feel a change in our physical and mental planes, but we also move into the spiritual plane.[119]

The Concept of Virtue and Vice

The human being is the best of the creation of God. The human body is the only vehicle for spiritual development and final beatitude. Even the gods crave for this body. But a human being has to undergo a discipline for the attainment of final emancipation.

Man is a social being, therefore, his actions not only pertain to his individual self, but are also related to society. As a created being he has also some relation with the Creator. Since a human being is a combination of human body and soul, he has not only to remain under physical discipline, but has also to follow certain moral laws. Thus an individual has to perform threefold duties *i.e.*
1. Duties for his self.
2. Duties in relation to society, and
3. Duties in relation to the Creator.

An individual who understands his duties in relation to self and society is a virtuous man. Regarding these duties or injunctions the verbal testimony plays a very important part. The virtues help in the attainment of bliss, therefore, the performance of duties not only constitute a step towards moral uplift, but also towards spiritual greatness.

In Sikhism, the performance of duty *i.e. dharma* does not mean the observance of the formal ritualism or the pursuance of the *Shastric* injunctions. The Sikh Gurus laid down a definite moral code, which enjoins a Sikh to do such actions which can be called higher *Karmas*. The practice of these higher *Karmas* is the practice of virtues in life. The social responsibility of an individual is the inception of these virtuous acts for the good of mankind.

Our mind tends more towards vices than virtues. We become slaves to the lust, anger, greed, worldly attachment and ego, which are the five great vices and are the root-cause of all the ills and foibles in life. They engender infirmities in individuals and societies. All sorts of troubles, anxieties, sorrows, frustrations, vexations and crosses crop up. In order to avoid such a miserable life, it is essential that an individual may bring himself under discipline.

The virtue and vice both are the creation of God. The *Satan*, if any, is subservient to the orders of the Lord. The physical and moral laws of causation work everywhere. The virtuous will be rewarded and the sinful punished. Vice is a sin. It is impure and unclean. God is pure. An individual becomes God-like to the extent he becomes pure.

In a world vitiated by all types of ills, one should avoid indulgence to the extreme and also avoid self-mortification to the extreme. Over-indulgence is sin, because it makes us materialists; over-repression is sin, because it misguides us towards fruitless mortification. On both the sides we lose balance. Sikhism follows the middle path *i.e.* the golden mean. It does not allow an individual either to renounce the world or to jump in the field like an unbridled horse.

The foremost duty of an individual is to understand *dharma* or the path of piety. The Pious is really great. This piety can be realised by the control over our senses. The five senses of sight, hearing, taste, smell and touch are to be kept under the following discipline:

1. Our sight should never become impure. We should

avoid a lustful and greedy look. We should look at the world as the creation of God, its beauty as the beauty of God. Our perception should be devoid of sense of possession, because it creates worldly attachment and ego.[120]
2. We should hear no evil. The faculty of hearing is related to the faculty of speech. Whatever we hear, it is the speech sound created by somebody. The hearing of evil can only be avoided, if we avoid a malicious speech. One should speak less in order to avoid any extravagant and unruly talk. The tongue often inflicts deep wounds than the sword. A discourteous talk creates unhealthy effect not only on the mind, but also on the body. The person who indulges in such talk receives punishment in the court of the Lord. We should be sweet in speech.[121]
3. One should not fall a prey to the tempting pleasures of the world. These pleasures are transitory and lead us to trouble. We like and indulge in whatever is tasteful. This is an age of *Kaliyuga* in which the tastes of the tongue and sex predominate. A true Sikh has to avoid all sensuous tastes and intoxicants.[122]
4. All smells inciting or exciting an individual to lustful acts are to be avoided.[123]

The above-mentioned injunctions, positive or negative must be practised in order to control the senses. These injunctions not only concern an individual, but have a social significance as well. The purity or perfection of an individual leads to the purity and perfection of society.

The Sikh Gurus have laid great emphasis on moral qualities in an individual. God as *Ishvara* is a treasure-house of qualities. If a *Jiva* practices these qualities, it becomes God-like. The ultimate objective of a Sikh is the unity with the Lord and this unity can be achieved by adopting His qualities and also remembering His Name. But our efforts in this direction can only be successful through the grace of a religious preceptor (Guru). Guru Nanak has said regarding these godly qualities that devotion (*Bhakti*) is not possible without these qualities.[124] Guru Arjan says:

From the toilet box of qualities, the fragrance should be taken out.

THE CONCEPT OF VIRTUE AND VICE

If these are qualities, O friend! we should share them. The qualities should be shared and the vices should be forsaken.[125]

The beauty aids of a personality suggested by **Guru Arjan** are truth, contentment, mercy and piety.[126]

The following godly qualities figure prominently in Sikh literature:

1. God is Truth.
2. God is Good.
3. God is Just.
4. God is Sweet.
5. God is Pure.
6. God is Fearless.
7. God is Devoid of Enmity.
8. God is Gracious.
9. God is Merciful.

If a *Jiva* adopts truth, goodness, justice, sweetness, purity, fearlessness, brotherly feelings, graciousness and mercifulness, he becomes godlike. These qualities prepare the ground for the realisation of Brahman.[127] They are like a base, over which a spiritual mansion can be raised.

The five major vices can be overcome with the practice of five virtues *i.e.* the lust can be overcome with self-control,[128] anger with toleration,[129] greed with contentment,[130] worldly affection with devotion to duty[131] and ego with modesty.[132] The sages have mentioned thirteen vices which are enemies of living beings. They are lust, anger, greed, dejection, delusion, cynicism, wrongful activity, envy, jealousy, irritated worry, malice scorn and fear.* These vices can be conquered with increasing control over mind, body and senses. Side by side they have talked of virtues:

"Forgiveness, self-possession, harmlessness, equality, truthfulness, straightforwardness, the conquest of senses, skill, gentleness, modesty, restfulness, absence of scorn, absence of excitement, sweet speech, harmlessness and absence of jealousy —of all these is self-control the source."**

Manu talks of ten virtues: "Self-possession, patience, self-control, integrity, purity, restraint, intelligence, learning,

---

* *Mahabharata,* Santi Parva, clxi, 1-3.
** *Mahabharata,* Santi Parva, clviii, (1), 13-16.

truthfulness, absence of anger—these are the marks of *dharma*"†
The Sikh Gurus also talk of all these virtues in an individual,
but they are bitterly against any barrier of caste in the society.
For them all the *Jivas* are equal and no barrier can be placed
between a man and a man, a man and a woman.

Sikh Gurus have laid great emphasis on the company of the
good (or *Sadh Sangat*) besides the above-mentioned virtues.[133]
In the company of the good one feels inspired for leading a
virtuous life. Guru Nanak considers humility or modesty as the
best quality in an individual.[134] By the practice of modesty we
can subdue ego which is the source of many evils. Modesty
inspires within us a holy sense of service[135] which leads us to
help others, to serve mankind, to serve all *Jivas*, and to serve
our country. The sense of service brings in mercy and
compassion toward others, produces the qualities of toleration,
forbearance, patience, and self-surrender.

With the armour of qualities and virtues, the Sikh enters the
field of action like a disciplined soldier and no enemy can stay
long before him. His actions are controlled by the injunctions
laid down by the great Gurus. He fulfils all his worldly duties,
but never forgets the Lord. He performs his physical, mental and
spiritual duties at the same time. He earns his livelihood,
performing his duty honestly. He takes out a portion of his
earning for the service of the needy brethren[136] and while
performing all the worldly duties, he remembers the Lord and in
the end attains the final beatitude.

The Concept of Ego

The *Vedas* declare that God is averse to ego or *Ahamkara*.[137]
The Gurus declare that the path of ego is averse to the path of
devotion. Modesty is a pre-requisite for the path of
devotion. The path of ego is the path of destruction.[138] Pride
hath a fall. Whoever thinks high of himself is reduced to dust
in a moment.[139]

† *Manu-smriti*, VI. 92.

THE CONCEPT OF EGO

The Ego (Pure) is the self-conceived as a non-empirical principle; it is ordinarily inaccessible to direct introspection, but inferred from introspective evidence.* There are two principal theories of Pure ego. The first is the soul theory which regards the pure ego as a permanent, spiritual substance underlying the fleeting succession of conscious-experience. The second theory is the transcendental theory of Kant which considers the self an inscrutable subject pre-supposed by the unity of empirical self-consciousness.* According to Guru Nanak the ego is the activity of self in duality or *maya*, as:

It comes in ego, goes in ego.
It is born in ego, it dies in ego.
It gives in ego, it loses in ego.
It benefits in ego, it takes in ego.
It is truthful and false in ego.
It thinks of virtue and sin in ego.
It goes to heaven and hell in ego.
It laughs in ego, it weeps in ego.
It is filthy in ego and clean in ego.
It loses its status in ego.
It is foolish in ego, it is wise in ego.
It is ignorant of liberation.
It is *maya* in ego, it is an illusion in ego
In ego the *Jivas* are created
When it realises ego, it realises the path.
Without knowledge it is led astray.
Under the *Hukm* of the Lord, our actions are scribed
The way we see ourselves, we visualise the *Hukm* of the Lord.[140]
Asa di Var, M. 1.

Endorsing the views of Guru Nanak about ego, **Guru Anged** says:

The ego is our self acting in ego.
It is enchained and transmigrates repeatedly.
Wherefrom this ego comes into being? How it is annihilated?
Under the *Hukm* of the Lord the ego is prepetuated by our action.
Ego is a dangerous disease, its treatment is also under this *Hukm*.
By the grace of the Lord the word of the Guru is practised.

*Dagobert D. Runes, *The Dictionary of Philosophy*, p. 88.

Hear O persons, saith Nanak, in this way the misery ceases.[141]
Asa di Var.

It becomes clear from the above quotations that in the field of *maya* the *Jiva* acts in ego. Whosoever rises above the fold of *maya* subdues his ego. *Maya* is not only wealth, but also the whole nature including the human nature as well, which works in duality. By renouncing wealth only one does not conquer ego. This ego has subdued the great sages of yore.[142]

Guru Nanak has accepted the *Samkhyan* principle of *Ahamkara*, through which the whole universe is born. When questioned by the yogis about the birth of the world, he clearly says that this world is created in ego. But he has also suggested a path for the extinction of this ego. The medium of escape from ego is the Name of the Lord.[143]

Guru Arjan has raised a direct question and also given a reply:

Is there anyone, who can break off this ego?
Who can divert this mind from this sweet ego?
The human being has become ignorant. He searches the unsearchable.
In this dark night, how can he see the light of the day?
He is tired of his wanderings and searches in various ways.
When the grace is showered, saith Nanak, he goes to *Sadh Sangat* (the company of the good) which is the treasure of happiness.[144]
Guari M.V.

Ego is the principle and subtle vice. It is always present in a *Jiva* in one form or another. It is the 'I' ness which spoils the fruit of great penances. The great *yogi* loses in a moment whatever he had gained through the self-mortification practised for hundred years. The Truth or the Fourth State is never realised in ego. The *Param Pad* is ego-less state.[145]

The Concept of Mind and intellect

Mind and intellect are the outer coverings of the soul undergoing transmigration. Mind is the product of *Rajasic Ahamkara*

THE CONCEPT OF MIND AND INTELLECT   57

alongwith five sensory and five motor organs. But *Ahamkara* itself is an evolute of *Mahat* or intellect. According to *Kathopanishad* body is the chariot, the soul is its master, the intellect is the charioteer, senses are the horses and the mind is the reins. Thus in the body-chariot the mind-reins are in the grip of intellect-charioteer. The immediate covering of the sheath of bliss (*anandmya kosh*) are the sheaths of intellect (*vigyanmaya kosh*) and mind (*manomaya kosh*). Thus mind and intellect have a closer and deeper relation with the soul (*Jivatman*).

In the region of effort (*Saram Khand*) in *Japji*, the mind and intellect are purified from the dirt of ego and a *Jiva* becomes a *Siddha*.[146] The dirt of ego gives a queer appearance to the mind. "The door of *Nirvana* is narrow, much narrower than the smallest seed, "says the Guru. "The mind has become an elephant, how can it pass through?"[147] The mind is puffed up with ego. But in its original form the mind is identical with *Jivatman*. The Guru says:

1. O mind, thou art light, realise thy source.[148]
2. This mind is *Aarsi*, some rare person sees in it.[149]

But the light of the mind is eclipsed by the dirt of ego, which has blackened it in the course of several births.[150] In order to control the mind, its reins should be tightened. It should be held tightly in the grip like the ends of churning rope.[151] Guru Arjan addresses the mind in the following manners:

O deceitful mind, thou canst not be trusted,
The ass is released only when the burden is placed on its
    back.[152]   *Bilawal*, M.V.

The mind here is likened to an ass, which should not be released until the burden of right intellect and the remembrance of the Lord is placed on its back. But it is not an easy job to bring the mind under control. The great sages have failed in their attempts. It always flies like a falcon.[153]

For the follower of mammon who works in duality, the mind
    is unconquerable.
He is always miserable and cannot find comfort even in a
    dream.
The *Pandits* are tired of studying at home, the *Siddhas* are
    tired of abstract meditation.

They are tired of their actions but the mind could not be brought under control.
The guisers are tired of their guises after a pilgrimage of sixty-eight holy places.
They could not know the mind and were illusioned by ego.
By the grace of the *Guru* the disciple was filled with the fear of the Lord. Fortunately the Lord dwelt in his mind.
With this fear the mind was brought under control and the ego was burnt with the word given by the Guru.[154]

Var Sorath, M. III.

When the disciple follows the discipline ordained by the Guru, he comes to know the nature of mind. He realises that the mind is like an intoxicated elephant and only the goad of the Guru can give it a new life.[155] The grace of the Lord and the Guru plays a great part in the conquest of mind.[156] When the mind is conquered, the Lord is realised and the whole world is conquered.[157] This is the real act of bravery. The Guru is very emphatic about the purity of mind. "Kabir says: my mind hath become pure like the waters of the *Ganges*. The Lord follows me calling "Kabir! Kabir!!""[158]

The intellect is mostly subdued by the mind. It is very difficult to get its release. The daily Sikh prayer lays great emphasis on the dictum: Let mind be subdued by the intellect.[159] Guru Ram Das addressed man of God thus:

O man of God! Do not follow the intelligence of mind.
It is of course difficult to do so.
Remember always the Name of the Lord and follow the intelligence of the true Guru.[160]

Bilawal, M. IV.

Guru Arjan prays for the gift of such intellect as may perpetuate the remembrance of the Lord.[161] Guru Nanak has defined the intellect in the following manner:

This is not intellect which is wasted in discussions and quarrels.
It is through intellect that we remember the Lord.
It is through intellect that we receive honours.
It is through intellect that we study and realize (the truth).
The intellect may be used while giving charity
This is the real path, saith Nanak, other things are *satanic*.[162]

Var Sarang, M.I.

The intellect makes us wise and educated. The education

makes us realise the truth. The Sikh Gurus are in favour of *Para Vidya* or the spiritual education. For them the verbal testimony is the vital source of knowledge. The Granth is the abode of the Lord.[163] All the education which creates ego is condemnable in their eyes. One who thinks about the principles of education through the grace of the Guru and studies, he is honoured[164] not only in this world, but also in the court of the Lord. This education creates such intellect as helps us to subdue the mind and realize the Lord.

The Concept of Death and life after Death

Death is a reality. Whatever is born, must die.[165] The bride of life will one day be taken away by the bridegroom of death.[166] Just as the peasant sows his field and lays his sickle to the crop at the harvesting time, whether the crop is mature or immature, in a similar way the sickle of death does not care for the *Jiva* of any age.[167] After day the night comes and after the night the day dawns. Time and tide wait for no man. There is no fixed time for death, neither the child, nor the youth nor the old escape it. That time is never known when *yama* throws its noose.[168] Every moment, which passes, reduces the span of our life. The *Jiva* does not realise it. The death as a rat is continuously cutting at the rope of life.[169]

The soul (*Jivatman*) is eternal. The death lays its hand only on the body, but nothing is destroyed. The air mixes in air, light in light, earth in earth. For what one should weep?[170] The Guru questions:

Who is dead? O who is dead?
Meet ye knowers of Brahman and discuss. A miracle hath
    happened.[171]   *Ramkali*, M. V

In the next moment the Guru himself replies:
He knows nothing of the life beyond death.
The one who weeps, also leaves the world.
Jiva is tied by illusions and worldly attachment,
Which becomes dream and the blind waggers.

The Creator has started this play.
The *Jiva* comes and goes under His *Hukm*.
Nothing dies nor anything is prone to death.
The *Jiva* does not die, it has to become eternal.
It is not, whatever you think of it.
Whoever knows it, I bow before him.
The Guru has removed my illusion, Saith Nanak
None dies, none comes and goes.[172] *Ramkali*, M. V.

The science talks of the indestructibility of matter and the same has been expounded here. But Gurus besides talking about the elements and their indestructibility talk also of light of the soul and Higher Soul.

Life and death are relative terms. The soul is life or consciousness. With soul the body is alive and without soul it is dead. The mind, intellect and vital breath are attached with the soul and not with the body. When the gross body (*Sthula Sarira*) dies, the subtle body of the soul consisting of the vital breath, mind and intellect lives. This subtle body of the soul also dies when the state of final emancipation is realised. Thus the term death only applies to the body, whether it is gross or subtle. The god of death or *yama* can destroy the body only.

After death the subtle body rises out of the gross body. The *Jiva* of this subtle body moves into the plane of those souls, which bear subtle bodies. In the *Adi Granth* it is written: "The dead meets the dead[173]" This means that the souls which leave the gross bodies of this world meet those souls which have already left their gross bodies in this world.

Nobody knows how death takes place. The subtle body going out of the gross body is never seen. None can point out the direction of its movement or the plane on which it settles.[174] Guru Nanak has propounded his thoughts about death in the following manner:

The body is dust; the air speaks (through it).
Tell, O wise man! who hath died;
The ego, quarrelsome nature and intellect have died.
The one that sees, hath not died,
... I have not died, my ignorance hath died.
The one that prevades hath not died ...... *Guari*, M. 1.[175]

Kabir talks of death also:

THE CONCEPT OF DEATH AND LIFE AFTER DEATH

> The death which hath frightened the whole world
> The word of the Guru hath enlightened me about that death,
> How should I die now? My mind understands (real) death.
> They die who have not known the Lord
> All talk about death
> But whoever dies in *Sehj* becomes immortal.
> My mind is in ecstacy, saith Kabir
> The illusion hath gone and the Lord remains (with me).[176]
> *Gauri, Kabir Ji.*

Kabir is emphatic on the point that none knows about his end.[177] Farid says: The falcon-death pounces upon its prey unexpectedly.[178] The death-end is like the slippery bank of the river.[179] As has been said above, one should try to understand death through the word of the Guru. One who understands, he never fears death.[180] Before death, he is in ecstasy and after death he merges in the Lord. Guru Amar Das says:

> Nothing do I know about my end, how shall I die?
> If the lord is not forgotton, the death will be easy.
> The world feareth death, everybody wants to live.
> By the grace of the Guru one dies while living, he
>   understands it in *Hukm*.
> If one dies such death, saith Nanak, he attains eternal life.[181]
> M. III; *Bihagra ki Var*, M. IV.

The Sikh Gurus believe in the theory of *karma* and transmigration. They often talk of the god of justice and his messengers. They also talk of Chitra and Gupta, who present the account of the individual's life before the god who is the sole deciding authority about the future of the soul. They also have given hints about heaven and hell. The good go to heaven and the bad are punished in hell. But the ideal presented by the Sikh Gurus and Bhagats and imbibed by a true devotee takes one much higher, where the god of justice has no approach[182] and where heaven and hell and even *Sukti* are rejected.[183]

The path that soul traverses after death is dark, difficult and hazarduous.[184] Much has been said about this path in the Puranas. According to Guru Arjan this path can be easily traversed with the light of the Name of the Lord.[185]

When a dear and near one departs, the kinsmen weep. A *siapa* is arranged and a great hue and cry is raised. This weeping has been condemned in the *Adi Granth*, because it is only due to the material losses on account of the death of an individual.[186]

When the soul appears before the god of Justice after death, a decision is taken about its future according to its actions in the material world. It may be sent to be re-born as an animal, a bird or an insect. It may even be sent to higher planes of gods according to its actions. It may be sent to be born as a human being again for its further development.

NOTES AND REFERENCES

[1]ब्रह्मा दीसै ब्रह्मा सुणीऐ . . . . . .   बिलावलु महला ५

[2]ओअंकारि ब्रह्मा उतपति । ओअंकारु कीआ जिनि चिति ।
ओअंकारि सैल जुग भए । ओअंकारि बेद निरमए ।
ओअंकारि सबद उधरे । ओअंकारि गुरमुखि तरे ।
ओनम अखर सुणहु बीचारु । ओनम अखरु त्रिभवण सारु ।१।
        रामकली महला १ दखण ओअंकारु

[3]तू अकाल पुरखु नाही सिरि काला
तू पुरखु अलेख अगंम निराला   मारू सोलहे महला १

[4]तू पारब्रह्मा परमेसरु . . . .   वार मारू २ महला ५

[5]अलख अपार अगंम अगोचर ना तिसु कालु न करमा ।
जाति अजाति अजोनी संभउ ना तिसु भाओ न भरमा ।१।
साचे सचिआर बिटहु कुरबाणु ।
ना तिसु रूप वरनु नही रेखिआ साचे सबदि नीसाण । रहाओ ।
ना तिसु मात पिता सुत बंधपु ना तिस कामु न नारी ।
अकुल निरंजन अपर परंपरु सगली जोति तुमारी ।२।
        सोरठि महला १

[6]एको एकु एकु हरि आपि ।   गौडी सुखमनी म: ५
तिसु बिनु दूसर होआ न होगु ।   गौडी सुखमनी म: ५

[7]किरतम ना.म कथे तेरे जिहवा ।
सतिनामु तेरा परा पूरबला ।   मारू म: ५.

[8]अरबद नरबद धुंधूकारा । धरणि न गगना हुकमु अपारा ।
ना दिनु रैनि न चंदु न सूरजु सुंन समाधि लगाइदा ।   मारू म: १

[9]जा तिसु भाणा ता जगतु उपाइआ ।   मारू म: १

[10]तू अकाल पुरख नाही सिरि काला ।   मारू सोलहे महला १

[11]एहु बिसु संसारु तुम देखदे एव हरि का रूपु है . . .   रामकली म:३, अनंदु

[12]ना ओहु मरता ना हम डरिआ । ना ओहु बिनसै ना हम कडिआ ।

ना क्रोहु निरधनु ना हम भूखे । ना ओसु दूखु न हम कउ दूखे ।१।
ना उसु बंधन ना हम बाधे । ना उस धंधा ना हम धांधे ।
ना उसु मैलु ना हम कउ मैला । ओसु आनंद त हम बद केला ।२।
ना उसु सोचु न हम कउ सोचा । ना उसु लेप न हम कउ पोचा ।
ना उसु भूख न हम कउ विसना । जा उहु निरमलु तां हम जचना ।३।

नानक गुरि खोए भ्रम भंगा । हम ओए मिलि होए इक रंगा ।४।   आसा महला ५

[13]आतमा परब्रह्मा का रूपु   गोंड महला ५
[14]मरणहारु एहु जीअरा नांहीं   गौंडी म: ५
[15]ना एहु मानसु ना एहु देउ । ना एहु जती कहावै सेउ ।
ना एहु जोगी ना अवधूता । ना इसु माए न काहू पूता ।१।
इआ मंदर महि कौन बसाई । तां का अंतु न कोऊ पाई ।१।   रहाओ
ना एहु गिरही न ओदासी । ना एहु राज न भीख मंगासी ।
ना इसु पिंडु न रकतू राती । ना एहु ब्रहमन ना एहु खाती ।२।
ना एहु तपा कहावै सेखु । ना एहु जीवै न मरता देखु ।
इसु मरते कउ जे कोई रोवै । जो रोवै सोई पति खोवै ।   गोंड कबीर

[16]अचरज कथा महा अनूपं । प्रातमा परब्रहमा का रूपु ।   रहाओ ।
ना एहु बूढा ना एहु बाला । ना इसु दूखु नही जम जाला ।
ना एहु बिनसै ना एहु जाए । आदि जुगादी रहिआ समाए ।१।
ना इसु उसनु नही इसु सीतु । ना इसु दुसमनु ना इसु मीतु ।
ना इसु हरखु नही इसु सोगु । सभ किछु इस का एहु करनै जोगु ।२।
ना इसु बापु नही इसु माइआ । एह अपरंपर होता आइआ ।
पाप पून का इसु लेपु न लागै । घट घट अंतरि सद ही जागै ।३।   गोंड महला ४

[17]उनकै संगि तेरी सभ बिधि थाटी ।
ओसु बिना तु होई है माटी ।
ओहू बैरागी मरे न जाए ।
हुकमे बांधा कार कमाए ।
जोडि विछोडै नानक थापि ।
अपनी कुदरति जाणै आपि ।   आसा महला ५

[18]धन करै विनउ दोऊ कर जोरे ।
प्रिअ परदेसि न जाहु वसहु घरि मोरे ।
ऐसा बणजु करहु ग्रिह भीतरि जितु उतरै भूख पिआसा हे ।४।
पिर कहिआ हउ हुकमी बंदा ।
ओहु भारो ठाकुर जिसु काणि न छंदा ।
जिचरु राखै तिचरु तुम संगि रहणा जा सदे त ऊठि सिधासा हे ।५।   मारू सोलहे महला ५

[19]उनकै संगि तु करती केल । उनके संगि हम तुम संगि मेल ।
उनके संगि तुम सभु कोऊ लोरै । ओसु बिना कोऊ मुखु नही जोरै ।२।

ते बैरागी कहा समाए । तिसु बिनु तुही दुहेरी री ।१।   रहाओ ।
उनकैं संगि तू ग्रिह महि माहरि । उनके संगि तू होई है ज.हर ।
उनकैं संगि तूं रखी पपोलि । ग्रोसु बिना तूं छुटकी रौलि ।२।
उनकैं संगि तेरा मानु पहुतु । उनकैं संग तुम साकु जगतु ।   आसा महला ५
²⁰ब्रह्मे ब्रह्मु मिलिआ कोइ न साकै भिंन करि बलिराम जीउ ।   सूही छंत महला ५

²¹एहु माइआ जितु हरि विसरे मोह उपजै माउ दूजा लाइग्रा ।
                                                            रामकली अनंद म: ३
²²एहु सरपनी ताकी कीती होई । बलु अबलु किग्रा इसते होई ।   आसा कबीर

²³निरगुनु आपि सरगुनु भी ग्रोही । कला धारि जिनि सगली मोही ।
                                                            गौढी सुखमनी म: ५

²⁴जिनि लाई प्रीति सोई फिरि खाइआ । जिन सुख देखालीं तिसु भउ बहुत दिखाइग्रा ।
भाई मीत कुटंब देख बिबादे । अउ आई वसिगत गुर परसादे ।
ऐसा देख बिमोहित होए ।
साधिक सिध मुरदेव मानुखा बिन साधू सभ द्रोहिन द्रोह ।
इक फिरहि उदासी तिन काम विआपे । इक संचहि गिरही तिन होइए न आपे ।
इक संतीकहावहि तिन बहुत कलपावै । हम हरि राखे लग सतिगुर पावै ।
तप करते तपसी भूलाए । पंडित मोहे लोभ सबाए ।
त्रैगुण मोहे मोहिग्रा आकास । हम सतगुर राखे देकर हाथ ।
गिग्रानी की होए वरती दास । कर जोढ सोबा करे अरदास ।
जो तूं कहें सु कार कमावा । जन नानक गुरमुख नेढ न ग्रावा ।   आसा महला ५

²⁵माइग्रा किसनो आखीग्रे किग्रा । माइग्रा करम कमाए ।
दुख सुख एह जीउ बध है हउमै करम कमाए ।   सिरी रागू ग्रसटपदो म: ३

²⁶एका माई जुगति विआई तिनि चेले परवाणु ।
इकु संसारी इकु भंडारी इक लाए दीबाणु ।
जिव तिस भावै तिवै चलावै जिव होवै फुरमाणु ।
ग्रोह् बेखै ग्रौना नदरि न ग्रावै बहुता एहु विडाणु ।   जपुजी

²⁷माथे त्रिकुटी द्रिसटि करूर । बोले कउढा जिहवा की फूढ ।
सदा भूखी पिर जानै दूर ।
ऐसी इस्त्री इक राम उपाई ।
उन सभ जग खाइग्रा हम गुर राखे मेरे भाई ।
पाऐ ठगुली सभ जग जोहिग्रा । ब्रह्मा बिसनु महादेउ मोहिआ ।   ग्रासां म: ५

²⁸सरपनी ते ऊपरि नही बलीग्रा ।
जिनि ब्रह्मा बिसनु महादेउ छलीग्रा ।   ग्रासा कबीर

²⁹माइग्रा होई नागनी जगति रही लपटाए ।
इस की सेवा जो करे तिस ही कउ फिरि खाए ।
गुरमुखि कोई गारढ तिनि मलि दलि लाई पांए ।

NOTES AND REFERENCES 65

नानक सोई उबरे जि सचि रहे लिव लाइ ।   वार गूजरी म: ३
30माइआ महि जिसु रखे उदासु ।
कहि कबीर हउ ताको दासु ।   भेरउ कबीर
31हहु माइआ की सोमा चार दिहाढे जादी विलम न होइ ।   आसा म: ३
32माइ बाप हित पूत भ्राता उन घर घर मेलिओ दूआ ।
किसही वाध घाट किस ही पहि सगले लर लर मूआ ।
हउ बलिहारी सतगुरु अपने जिन एहु चलित दिखाइआ ।
गूभी माहि जले संसारा भगत न विआपै माइआ ।   धनासरी महला ५
33राज कमाइ करी जिन थैली ता कै संग न चंचल चलीआ ।   मारू महला ५
34माइआधारी अति अंना बौला ।   गौंढी की वार म: ३

35अरबद नरबद धुंदूकारा । धरणि न गगना हुकम अपारा ।
ना दिन रैण न चंद न सूरज सुंन समाधि लगाइदा ।
ना तिस भाणा ता जगत उपाइआ । बाभ कला आडाण रहाइआ ।
ब्रह्मा बिसन महेश उपाइ माइआ मोह वधाइदा ।   मारू सोलहे म: १
36जब ओंकारु एहु कछु न द्रिसटेता । पाप पुंन तब कह ते होता ।
जब धारी आपन सुंन समाधि । तब बैर बिरोध किसु संगि कमाति ।
जब इस का बरनु चिहनु न जापत ।
तब हरख सोग कहु किसहि बिआपत ।
जब आपन आप आपि पारब्रह्म । तब मोह कहा किस होवत भरम । ...
आपन खेलु आप वरतीजा । नानक करनैहार ना दूजा । १ ।
जह आपि रचिओ परपंचु आकारु । तिहु गुण महि कीनो बिसथारु ।
पाप पुंन तह मई कहावत । कोऊ नरक कोऊ सुरग बंछावत ।
आल जाल माइआ जंजाल । होमे मोह भरम में भार ।
दूख सूख मान अपमान । अनिक प्रकार कीओ बखान ।
आपन खेलु आप करि देखै । खेलु संकोचै तउ नानक एकै । ७ ।
   गौढी सुखमनी म: ७
37वेल न पाईआ पंडती जि होवै लेखु पुराणु ।
वखतु ना पाइिओ कादीआ जि लिखणि लेखु कुराणु ।
थिति वारु न जोगी जाणै रुति माहु न कोई ।
जा करता सिरठी कउ साजे आपेजाणे सोई ।   जपुजी
38छतीह जुग गुबारु करि वरतिआ सुंना हरि ।   राकली वार ३
39सगल समिग्री एकस घट माहि । अनिक रंग नाना द्रिसटाहि ।   गौढी महला ५
40एह सरपनी ताकी कीती होई । बलु अबलु किआ इस ते होई ।   आसा कबीर
41सिव सकति आपि उपाइके करता आपे हुकम तरताए ।   रामकली म: ष अनंदु
42इकसु ते होइिओ अनंता नानक एकसु माहि समाइ जीउ ।   माभ म: ५
43कितु कितु बिधि जग उपजै पुरखा
कितु कितु दुखु बिनसि जाई ।
हउमें विच जग उपजै पुरखा
नामि विसरिऐ दुखु पाई ।   रामकली महला १ सिध गौसटि

⁴⁴प्रधान पुरखु परगट सभ लोएि । गौड़ी सुखमनी महला ५
⁴⁵माता धरती महतु . . . . . जपुजी
तीनि गुणा एिक सकति उपाएिआ ।
महा माएिआ ताकी है छाएिआ । गौंड म: ५
⁴⁶साचे ते पवना मएिआ पवने ते जल होएि ।
जल ते त्रिभवण साजिआ घट घट जोत समोएि । सिरी राग महला १
⁴⁷उतपति परलउ सबदे होवै ।
सबदे ही फिरि ओपति होवे । माझ म: ३
⁴⁸नाम के धारे सगले जंति । नाम के धारे खंड ब्रहिमंड । गौड़ी सुखमनी म: ५
⁴⁹कीता पसाउ एको कवाउ ।
तिस ते होएि लख दरीआउ । जपुजी
⁵⁰पवणु गुरु पाण पिता माता धरति महतु ।
दिवसु राति दुएि दाई दाएिआ खेलै सगल जगतु । जपुजी
⁵¹एका माई जुगति विआई तिन चेले परवाणु ।
एिकु संसारी एिकु भंडारी एिकु लाए दीबाणु । . . . .
ओहु वेखै ओना नदरि ना आवै बहुता एहु विडाणु । जपुजी
⁵² . . . . केते कानह महैस ।
केते बरमे घाढति घढीअहि रूप रंग के वेस । जपुजी
⁵³पाताला पाताल लख आगासा आगास । जपुजी
⁵⁴कई कोटि खाणी अर खंड । । गौड़ी सुखमनी म: ५
कई कंटि आकास ब्रहिमंड ।
⁵⁵अंतु न जापै कीता आकारु ।
अंतु न जापै पारावारु । जपुजी
⁵⁶केतीआ खाणी केतीआ बाणी केते पात नरिंद ।
केतीआ सुरती सेवक केते नानक अंतु ना अंतु । जपुजी
⁵⁷तिथै खंड मंडल वरभण्डु ।
जे को कथै ता अंत ना अंतु । जपुजी
⁵⁸नानक रचना प्रभु रची बहु बिधि अनिक प्रकार । गौड़ी सुखमनी म: ५
⁵⁹बएिआलीस लख जी जल माहि होते . . . . . आसा नामदेव
⁶⁰सचे तेरे खंड सचे ब्रहिमंड ।
सचे तेरे लोअ सचे आकार । आसा दी बार-सलोक म: १

⁶¹कायउ देवा काएिअउ देवल काएिग्रउ जंगम जाती ।
काएिअउ धूप दीप नईबेदा काएिग्रउ पूजउ पाती । १ ॥
काएिआ बहु खंड खोजते नवनिधि पाई ।
ना कछु आएिबो ना कछु जाएिबो राम की दुहाई । १ ।
जो ब्रहमंड सोई पिंडे जो खोजै सो पावै ।
पीपा प्रणव परमततु है सतिगुरु होएि लखावै । धनासरी पीपा
⁶²इढा पिगुला और सुखमना तीनि बसहि एिक ठाई ।
बेणी संगमु तह पिरागु मनु मजनु करे तिथाई । १ ।

NOTES AND REFERENCES 67

संतहु तहा निरंजन रामु है ।
गुर गमि चीनै बिरला कोई । तहां निरंजनु रमईआ होइ । १ । रहाओ ।
देव सथाने किआ नीसाणी । तह बाजे सवदि अनाहद बाणी ।
तह चंदु न सूरजु पउणु न पाणी । साखी जागी गुरमुखि जाणी । २ ।
उपजै गिग्रानु दुरमति छीजै । अमृत रसि गगनंतरि भीजै ।
एस कला जो जाणै मेउ । तासु भेटै परम गुरदेउ । ३ ।
दसम दुआरा अगम अपारा परम पुरख की घाटी ।
उपरि हाटु हाट परि आला आले भीतरि थाती । ४ ॥
जागतु रहै सु कबहू न सोवै । तीनि तिलोक समाधि पलोवै ।
बीज मंत्र लै हिरदै रहै । मनूआ उलटि सुंन महि गहै । ५ ।
जागतु रहै न अलीआ भाखै । पाचउ इंदी बसि करि राखै ।
गुर की साखी राखै चीति । मनु तनु अरपे क्रिसन परीति । ६ ।
कर पलव साखा बीचारे । अपना जनमु न जूऐ हारे ।
असुर नदी का बंधै मूलु । पछिम फेर चढावै सूरु ।
अजरु जरे सु निभर भरै । जगंनाथ सिउ गोसटि करै । ७ ।
चउमुख दीवा जोति मुझार । पलू अनक मूलु बिचकारि ।
सरब कला ले आपे रहै । मनु माणकु रतना महि गुहै । ८ ।
मसतकि पदमु दुआलै मणी । माहि निरंजनु त्रिभवण धणी ।
पंच सबद निरमाइल बाजे । ढुलके चवर संख धन गाजे ।
दलि मलि दैतहु गुरमुखि गिआनु । बेणी जाचै तेरा नामु । ९ ॥   रामकली बेणी

[63]तब आतमै कहिआ, "ब्रहमंड बिखै चंद अर सूरज हैं । इस पिंड मीह कहां हैं?"
तब प्रातमै कहिआ, 'एहु जो नेत्र हैं, इनही को उजीआरा है ।'
तब प्रातमै कहिआ 'चंद अर सूरज की प्रकित है, कबहू चांदना होता है ।
कबहू अंधिआरा होता है ।'
तब प्रातमै कहिआ, 'जब निदरा आवती है, तब 'अंधिआरा होता है । जद उधड़ते हैं,
तो चांदना होता है ।'
तब प्रातमै कहिआ, "ब्रहिमंड महि अठसठ तीरथ हैं । इस पिंड महि कहां हैं ?"
तब प्रातमै कहिआ, जो कछु सुकृति करता है । सो एहु अठसठ तीरथ समान है।"
तु प्रातमै कहिआ, ब्रहमंड बिखे नरक अर सुरग हैं । इस पिंड महि कहां हैं?'
तु प्रातमै कहिआ, 'जब दुख लगता है, तब नरक है । जब सुख लागे तब सुरग हैं।"
                                       जो ब्रहिमंडे सोई पिंडे-प्राण संगली

[64]इसु काइआ अंदर वसतु असंखा ।
गुरमुखि साचु मिलै ता वेखा ।
नउ मरवाजे दमवैं मुकता अनहद सबदु वजावणिआ । ३ ।   माझ महला ३
[65]इसु काइआ अंदर बहुतु पसारा ।
नामु निरंजनु अति अगम अपारा ।
गुरमुखि होवै सोई पाए आपे बखसि मिलावणिआ । २ ।   माझ महला ३
[66]काइआ अंदरि सभु किछु वसै खंड मंडल पाताला ।   ...
काइआ अंदरि रतन पदारथ भगति भरे भंडारा ।
इसु काइआ अंदरि नउखंड प्रिथमी हाट पटण बाजारा ।

इसु काइआ अंदरि नासु नउनिधि पाईऐ गुर के सबदि वीचारा ।४।..
काइआ अंदरि भउ भाउ वसै गुर परसादी पाई ।६।...
काइआ अंदरि ब्रह्मा बिसनु महेसा सभ ओपति जितु संसारा ।...
सूही म: ३

67इस काइआ की कीमति किनै ना पाई ।
मेरे ठाकुरि एह बणत बणाई ।
गुरमुखि होवै सु काइआ सोधै आपहि आपु मिलाइदा । मारू म: ३

68करम धरती सरीर जुग अंतर जो बोवै सो खात ।   सिरी राग महला ५
69जेहा बीजै सो लुणे करमा संदा खेत ।   बारहमाह माझ महला ५
70दद्दे दोसु न देउ, किसै दोसु करंमा आपणिआ ।
जो मै कीआ सो मै पाइआ दोस ना दीजै अवर जना । आसा पटी महला १
71सचै मारगि चलदिआ उसतति करे जहान ।   बारहमाहा माझ महला ५
सोई कंम कमाइ जित मुख उजला ।   आसा महला ५
72उतम से दर उतम कहीअहि नीच करम बहि ऐए ।   सिरी रागु महला १
73करे दुहकरम दिखावै होर । राम की दरगह बाधा चोर । गौड़ी महला ५
मंदे अमल करंदिआ एहु सजाइ तिनाह ।   सलोक फरीद
74खाए खाऐ करे बदफैली जाणु विसू की बाड़ी जीउ । माझ म: ५
75जिह कारण होवहि सरमिंदा एहा कमानी रीत ।
संत की निंदा साकत दी पूजा ऐसी द्रिड़ी बिपरीत ।   धनासरी महला ५
76फरीदा जिनी कंमी नाहिगुण ते कंमड़े विसार ।
मत सरमिंदा थीवई सांई दै दरबार ।   सलोक फरीद
77जो धुरि लिखिआ लेख सो करम कमाइसी ।
लेख न मिटई हे सखा जो लिखिआ करतार ।   गूजरी महला ३
दखण ओअंकार-रामकली महला १

78करमबधु तुम जीउ कहत हो करमहि किनि जीउ दीनु रे । गौंड कबीर
79अलह भावै सो भला ता लभी दरबार ।   शेख फरीद
80. . . . सुखु रोगु भइआ . . . .   वार आसा महला १
81सिआनप काहूं कामि न आत ।
जो अनुरूपिओ ठाकुर मेरे होइ रही उह बात ।   गूजरी महला ५
82नानक जिसनो नदरि करेइ । अमृत नामु आपे देइ ।
बिखिआ की बासना मनहि करेइ । आपणा भाणा आप करेइ । बसंतु महला ३
83जह आपि रचिउ परपंचु अकार ।
तिहु गुण महि कीनो बिसथार ।   गौड़ी सुखमनी महला ५
84सुरग बासु न बाछीऐ डरीऐ न नरक निवास ।   गौड़ी कबीर
85कवनु नरकु किआ सुरगु बिचारा संतन दोऊ रादे ।
हम काहू की कारणि न कढते अपने गुर परसादे ।   रामकली कबीर
86कबीर सुरग नरक ते मैं रहिओ सतगुर के परसादि ।
चरन कमल की मउज महि रहउ अंत अरु आदि ।   सलोक कबीर
87आगै विमल नदी अगनि बिख झेला ।

NOTES AND REFERENCES 69

तिथै अवरु न ई जीउको इकेला ।
भड भड अगनि सागरु दे लहरी पड़ि दझहि मनमुखताई है ।   मारू महला १
88ई जनम भए कीट पतंगा । कई जनम गज मीन कुरंगा ।
कई जनम पंखी सरप होएश्रो । कई जनम हैवर ब्रिख जोएश्रो । १ ।
मिलु जगदीस मिलन की बरीआ । चिरंकाल एह देह संजरीआ । १ ।   रहाओ
कई जनम सैल गिरि करिआ । कई जनम गरभ हिरि खरिआ ।
कई जनम साख कर उपाइआ । लख चउरासीह जोनि भ्रमाइआ । २ ।
                                                                                              गौड़ी गुआरेरी महला ५
86मेरी मेरी धारी । ओहा पेरि लोहारी ।   मारू महला ५
90हउ हउ करम कमाणे । तेते बंध गंलाणे ।   मारू महला ५
91तिसना अगनि जलै संसारा । लोभु अभिमानु बहुतु अहंकारा ।
घरि घरि जनमै पति गवाए अपणी बिरथा जनम गवावणिआ ।
                                                                                              माझ महला ३-१२०
92जनम मरन के मिटे अंदेसे । साधू के पूरन उपदेसे ।
थिति पाई चूके भ्रम गवन । सुनि नानक हरि हरि जसु स्रवन ।
                                                                                              गौड़ी सुखमनी मः ५
93अंतिकालि जो लछमी सिमरै ऐसी चिंता महि जे मरै ।
सरप जोनि वलि वल अऊतरे । १ ।
अंतिकालि जो इस्त्री सिमरै ऐसी चिंता महि जे मरे ।
बेसवा जोनि वलि वल अउतरै । २ ।
अंतिकालि जो लडिके सिमरै ऐसी चिंता महि जे मरे ।
सूकर जोनि बलि वल अउतरे । ३ ।
अंतिकालि जो मंदर सिमरै ऐसी चिंता महि जे मरे ।
प्रेत जोनि वलि वल अउतरे । ४ ।   गूजरी त्रिलोचन

94हुकमी होवनि आकार हुकमु न कहिआ जाई ।
हुकमी होवनि जीअ हुकमि मिलै वडिआई ।
हुकमी उत्तम नीचु हुकमि लिखि दुख सुख पाईअहि ।
इकना हुकमी बखसीस इकि हुकमी सदा मवाईअहि ।
हुकमै अंदरि सभु को बाहिरि हुकम ना कोए ।
नानक हुकमै जे बुझे त हउमैं कहैं न कोए । २ ।   जपुजी
95गला उपरि तपावसु न होवई विसु खाधी ततकालि मरि जाए ।
भाई बेखहु निआउ सचु करते का जेहा कोई करे तेहा कोई पए......
                                                                          गौड़ी की वार महला ४-सलोक महला ४
96केतिआ दूख भूख सद मार ।
एहि भि दाति तेरी दातार ।   जपुजी
97वेखै विगसै करि वीचारु ।   जपुजी
98 . . . वरतै ताको ताक ।   आसा दी वार
99हरि जो किछु करे सु हरि किआ भगता भाएिआ ।   गौड़ी महला ५
100भाणा मंने सदा सुख होए ।

नानक सच समावै सोइ ।   आसा महला ३

[101]जो तुध करणा सो करि पाइआ । भाणे विचि को विरला आइआ ।
भाणा मंने सो सुखु पाए भाणे विचि सुखु पाइंदा । १ । ...
मनमुख अंधु करे चतुराई । भाणा न मंने बहुत दुख पाई ।
भरमे भूला आवै जावै भरु महलु न कबहू पाइंदा । ५ ।

                                                              मारू महला ३

[102]हुकमे धारि अधर रहावै । हुकमै उपजै हुकमि समावै ।
हुकमे ऊच नीच बिउहार । हुकमे अनिक रंग प्रकार ।   गौड़ी सुखमनी म: ५

[101]हुकमै अंदरि निमिआ पिआरे हुकमै उदर मझारि ।
हुकमै अंदरि जंमिआ पिआरे ऊधउ सिर कै भारि ।
गुरमुख दरगह जाणीए पिआरे चलै कारज सारि ।
हुकमे अंदरि आया पिआरे हुकमे जादो जाए ।
हुकमे बंनि चलाईए पिआरे मनमुखि लहै सजाए ।
हुकमे सबदि पछाणीए पिआरे दरगह पैधा जाए ।
हुकमे गणत गणाईए पिआरे हुकमे हउमै दोइ ।
हुकमे भवै भवाईए पिआरे अवगणि मुठी रोइ ।
हुकम सिंञापै साह का पिआरे सच मिलै वडिआई होइ ।   सोरठि महला १

[103]सचा सउदा विरला को पाए । पूरा सतिगुर मिलै मिलाए ।
गुरमुखि होए सु हुकमु पछाणे माने हुकमु समाइदा । ९ ।
हुकमे आइआ हुकमि समाइआ । हुकमै दीसै जगतु उपाइआ ।
हुकमे सुरगु मछु पइआला हुकमै कला रहाइदा । १० ।
हुकमे धरती धउल सिरि भारे । हुकमे पउण पाणी गैणारे ।
हुकमे सिव सकती घरि वासा हुकमे खेल खेलाइदा । ११ ।
हुकमे आडाणे आगासी । हुकमे जल थल त्रिभवण वासी ।
हुकमे सास गिरास सदा फुनि हुकमे देखि दिखाइदा । १२ ।
हुकमि उपाए दस अवतारा । देव दानव अगणत अपारा ।
मानै हुकमु सु दरगह पैझै सचि मिलाए समाइदा ।१३।
हुकमे जुग छतीह गुदारे । हुकमे सिध साधिक बीचारे ।
आपि नाथ नाथी सभ जाकी बखसे मुकति कराइदा ।१४।   मारू महला १

[104]प्रभ मिलणे की एव नीसाणी ।
मनि इको सचा हुकमु पछाणी ।   माझ महला ५

[106]सभ तेरी कुदरति तूं कादिरु करता पाकी नाई पाकु ।
नानक हुकमै अंदरि वैखै वरतै ताको ताकु ।   वार आसा महला १

[107]एको नामु हुकमु है ......   सिरी रागु महला १

[108]करमी आवै कपड़ा नदरी मोखु दुआरु ।   जपुजी
[109]एहु पिरम पिआला खसम का जेहि भावै तेहि देइ ।   रामकली वार ३
[110]सहु मेरा एक दूजा नहीं कोई । नदर करे मेलावा होई ।

                                                              आसा महला १

[111]करमु होवै ता परमपद पाईऐ कथै अकथ कहाणी ।
तूं करता कीआ सभ तेरा किआ को करे पराणी ।   आसा महला ३
[112]नदर करे जिसु आपणी तिसनो भावनी लाए ।
सत संतोख एहु संजमी मन निरमल सबद सुणाए ।   आसा महला ३
[113]नदरि करहि जे आपणी ता नदरी सतिगुर पाइआ ।   आसा दी वार महला १
[114]नदरी सतगुरू सेवीऐ नदरी सेवा होइए ।
नदरी एहु मनु वसि आवै नदरी मन निरमलु होइए ।   वडहंस म: ३
[115]सचु सदा है निरमला भाई निरमल सचे सोइए ।
नदरि करे जिसु आपणी भाई तिसु परापति होइए ।   सोरठि महला ५
[116]नदरि करे ता एहु मोहु जाइए ।
नानक हरि सिउ रहे समाइए ।   आसा महला १
[117]जैसी नदरि करे तैसा होइए ।
विण नदरि नानक नही कोइए ।   धनासरी महला १
[118]नदरि करे चूकै अभिमानु ।   बसंत महला ३
[119]नदरि करे ता हरि रसु पावै ।
नानक हरि रस हरि गुण गावै ।   सूही महला ४

[120]ए नेत्रहु मेरिओ हरि तुम महि जोति धरी हरि बिनु अवरु न देखहु कोई ।
                                                  रामकली म : २ अनंद
[121]ए सरवणहु मेरिहो साचै सुनणे ने पठाए । . . . .
कहै नानकु अंम्रित नामु सुणहु पवित्र होवहु साचै सुनणो नो पठाए ।
                                                  रामकली महला ३ अनंद
[122]बहु सादहु दूख परापति होवै । भोगहु रोग सु अति विगोवै ।   मारू म: १
जेतै रस सरीर के तेते लगहि दुख ।   वार मलार म: १
झूठा मद मूल न पीजै जेका पार वसाए ।   वार बिगाडड़ा म: ३
[123]लोभ लहिर सभ सुआन हलक हैं हलकिओ सभहि बिगारे ।   नट महला ४
[124]विणु गुण कीते भगति न होइए ।   जपुजी
[125]गुण का होवै वासला कढ वास लईजै ।   सूही महला १
जे गुण होवन साजना मिल साझ करीजै ।
साझ करीजैं गुणह केरी छोड अवगुण चलीऐ । . . . . . . सूही महला १
[126]सत संतोख दइआ धरम सीगार बनावउ ।   बिलावलु म: ५
[127]गुण की सांझ सुख ऊपजै सची भगति करेन ।   सूही असटपदी महला ३
[128]परधन परदारा परहरी । ताकै निकटि बसै नरहरी ।
                                                  भैरउ नामदेउ
[129]दरबेसां नौ लोडीऐ रुखां दी जीरांदि ।   सलोक फरीद
[130]बिना संतोख नही कोऊ राजै ।   गौड़ी सुखमनी म: ५
[131]कबीर जउ ग्रिह करहि त धरभु करु नही त करु बैरागु ।   सलोक कबीर
[132]आपस कउ जो जानै नीचा । सोउ गनीऐ सभ ते ऊचा ।   गौड़ी सुखमनी म: ५
[133]सतसंगति सतगुर चाटसल है जितु हरि गुण सिखा ।   वार कानड़ा म: ४

134मिठत नीवी नानका गुण चंगिआईआं ततु ।   आसा दी वार म: १
135सेवा करत होइ निहकामी । तिस कउ होत प्रापति सुआमी ।
   गौड़ी सुखमनी म: ५
136घालि खाइ किछु हथहु देइ । नानक राहु पछाणहि सेइ ।   वार सारग म: १

137हरि जीउ अहंकारु न भावई वेद कूकि सुणावहि ।   वार मारु म: ३
138अभिमानी की जड़ सरपर जाइ ।   गौडं म: ५
139जे जे बहुत करे अहंकारि । ओहु खिन महि रुलता खाकू नाल ।   गोंड म: ५
140हउ विचि आइआ हउ विच गइआ ।
   हऊ विचि जंमिआ हउ विच मुआ ।
   हउ विचि दिता हउ विचि लिआ ।
   हउ विचि खटिआ हउ विचि गइआ ।
   हउ विचि सचिआरु कूड़िआरु ।
   हउ विचि पाप पु‍न वीचारु ।
   हउ विचि नरकि सुरगि अवतारु ।
   हउ विचि हसै हउ विचि रोवे ।
   हउ विचि भरीऐ हउ विचि धोवे ।
   हउ विचि जाती जिनसी खोवै ।
   हउ विचि मूरखु हउ विचि सिआणा। ।
   मोख मुकति की सार न जाणा ।
   हउ विचि माइआ हउ विचि छाइआ ।
   हउमै करि करि जंत उपाइआ ।
   हउमै बूझे ता दरु सूझे ।
   गिआन विहूणा कथि कथि लूझै ँ ।
   नानक हुकमी लिखीऐ लेखु ।
   जेहा वेखहि तेहा वेखु ।
   सलोक म: १- आसा दी वार
141हउमै एहा जाति है हउमै करम कमाहि ।
   हउमै एई बंधना फिरि फिरि जोनी पाहि ।
   हउमै किथहु उपजै कितु संजमि एह जाइ ।
   हउमै एहो हुकमु है पइऐ किरति फिराहि ।
   हउमै दीरघ रोगु है दारू भी इसु माहि ।
   किरपा करे जे आपणी ता गुर का सबदु कमाहि ।
   नानक कहै सुणहु जनहु इतु संजमि दुख जाहि ।   आसा दी वार म: २
142माइआ तजी त किआ भइआ जउ मान तजिआ नहि जाए ।
   मान मुनी मुनिवर गले मान सभै कउ खाए ।   सलोक कबीर
143हउमै विच जगु उपजै पुरखा
   नाम विसरिऐ दुखु पाई ।   सिध गोसटि-रामक ली म: १
144है कोई ऐसा हउमै तोरै ।
   इस मीठी ते एहु मन होरै ।

अगिआनी मानुख भएआ जो नाही सो लोरै ।
रैण अंधारी कारीआ कवन गुणति जित भोरै ।
भ्रमतो भ्रमतो हारिआ अनिक बिधी कर टोरै ।
कहु नानक किरपा भई साधु संगति निधि मोरै ।   गौड़ी म: ५
[145]हउ हउ करत नही सचु पाईऐ ।
हउमै जाए परमपद पाईऐ ।   गौडी म: १

[146]तिथै घड़ीऐ सुरति मति मनि बुधि ।
तिथै घड़ीऐ सुरा सिधा की सुधि ।   जपजी
[147]कबीर मुकति भुग्आरा संकुरा राई दसऐं भाए ।
मनु तउ मैगलु होइ रहिउ निकसो किउ कै जाए ।   सलोक कबीर
[148]मन तूं जोति सरूप है अपना मूल पछाण ।   आसा म: ३
[149]एहु मन आरसी कोई विरला देखै ।   माझ अस्टपदी म: ३
[150]जनम जनम की इसु मन कउ मलु लागी काला होआ सिआहु ।
                                                   वार सोरठि म: ४-सलोक म: ३
[151]एहु मनु ईटी हाथि करहु . . . . .   राग सूही महला १
[152]मन खुटहर तेरा नहि बिसासु तूं बहु उनमादा ।
खरका पैखर तउ छुटै जउ ऊपर लादा ।   बिलावस म: ५
[153]वसि आणिहु वे जन इस मनु कउ
मनु बासे जिउ नित मउदिआ ।   सूही छंत महला ४
[154]मनमुख मन अजित है दूजे लगे जाए ।
तिस नो सुख सुपने नही दुखै दुख विहाए ।
घरि परि पड़ पड़ पंडित थके सिध समाधि लगाए ।
एह मन वसि न आवई थके करम कमाए ।
भेखधारी भेख कर थके अठसठ तीरथ नाए ।
मन की सार न जाणनी हउमै भरमि भुलाए ।
गुरपरसादी भउ पएआ वडभाग वसिआ मन आए ।
भै पएऐ मन वसि होआ हउमै सबद जलाए ।   वार सोठि म: ३
[155]मन कुंचर काएआ उदिआनें ।
गुरु अंकुस सबद सच नीसानैं ।   गौड़ी अस्टपदी म: १
[156]मन वसि आवै नानका जे पूरन किरपा होए ।   गौड़ी थिती म: ५
[157]मनूआ जीते हरि मिलै एह सूरतण वेस ।   गौड़ी बावन अखरी म: ५
मन जीतै जग जीत ।   जपुजी
[158]कबीर मन निरमल भएआ जसा गंगा नीर ।
पाछै लागो हरि फिरै कहत कबीर कबीर ।   सलोक कबीर
[159]मन नीवां रहे, मत उची रहे ।   अरदास
[160]मन की मति तिआगहु हरिजन एहा बात कठैनी ।
अनदिन हरि हरि नाम धिआबहु गुरु सतगुरु की मति लैनी । बिलावल महला ४
[161]सा बुधि दीजै जितु बिसरहि नाही । सा मति दीजै जितु तुध धिआई ।   माझ महला
[162]अकल एह न आखीऐ अकल गवाईऐ बाद ।

अकली साहिब सेबीऐ अकली पाईऐ मान ।
अकली पड़ के बुझीऐ अकली कीचै दान ।
नानक आखै राहु एह होर गला सैतान ।   वार सारंग म: १

163पोथी परमेसुर का थान ।   सारंग म: ५
164गुरपरसादी विदिआ वीचारै पड़ पड़ पावै मान ।   प्रभाती महला १

165जो उपजै सो काल संघारिआ ।   गौड़ी असटपदी म: १
जो जनमै सो जानहु मूआ ।   आसा महला ५
सभना मरना आइआ ।   वडहंस म: १
166जिंद बहुटी मरणु वर लै जासी परणाए ।   सलोक फरीद
167जैसे किरसाण थोबै किरसाणी ।
काची पाकी वाढ पराणी ।   आसा म: ५
168ओह बेरा नहि बूझीऐ जउ आए परै जमकंधु ।   गौड़ी बावन अखरी म: ५
169दिवस चड़ै फिर आथवै रैण सबाई जाए ।
आव घटै नर न बूझै नित मूसा लाज टुकाए ।   सिरी राग महला ४
170पवनै महि पवनु समाइआ ।
जोती महि जोति रल जाइआ ।
माटी माटी होई एक ।
रोवनहारे की कवन टेक ।   रामकली म: ५
171कउनु मूआ रे कउन मूआ ।
ब्रह्म गिआनी मिलि करहु वीचारा एहु तउ चलतु भइआ ।   रामकली म: ५
172अगली किछु खबरि न पाई । रोवनहारु भि ऊठि सिधाई ।
भरम मोह के बांधे बंध । सुपनु भइआ मखलाए बंध । २ ।
एहु तउ रचनु रचिआ करतारि । आवतु जावत हुकमि अपारि ।
नह को मूआ न मरणे जोगु । नह बिनसै अबिनासी होगु । ३ ।
जो एहु जाणहु सो एहु नाहि । जांणनहारे कउ बलि जाउ ।
कहु नानक गुर भरमु चुकाइआ । ना कोई मरै न आवै जाइआ ।४। रामकली म: ५
173जीवते कउ जीवता मिलै मूए कउ मूआ ।   वार सूही म: ३-सलोक म: २
174जाते जाइ कहा ते आवै ।
कह उपजै कत जाइए समावै ।   गौड़ी महला १
175देही माटी बोलै पउणु । बुझु के गिआनी मूआ है कउणु ।
मूई सुरति बादु अहंकारु । ओहु न मूआ जो देखणहारु ।२। . . . .
हउ न मूआ मेरी मुई बलाए । ओहु न मूआ जो रहिआ समाए ।   गौड़ी म: १
176जिह मरनै सभ जगतु तरासिआ ।
सो मरना गुर सबदि प्रगासिआ ।१।
अब कैसे मरउ मरनि मनु मानिआ ।
मरि मरि जाते जिन रामु न जानिआ ।१। रहाआं ।
मरनो मरनु कहै सभु कोई ।
सहजे मरे अमरु होए सोई ।२।
कहु कबीर मन भइआ अनंदा ।

गएिआ भरमु रहिआ परमानंदा ।३।   गौड़ी कबीर जी
[177]कबीर मरता मरता जग मूआ मरि भि न जानै कोिए ।   सलोक कबीर
[178]केल करेंदे हंझ नौ अचिंते बाज पए ।   सलोक फरीद
[179]मउतै दा बंना एवै दिसै जिउ दरीआवै ढाहा ।   सलोक फरीद
[180]जिह मरनैं ते जग डरै मेरै मन आनंद ।   सलोक कबीर
[181]किआ जाणा किव मरहिगे कैसा मरणा होिए ।
जेकरि साहिब मनहु न वीसरै ता सहिला मरणा होिए ।
मरणे ते जगतु डरै जीविआ लोड़ै सभु कोिए ।
गुर परसादी जीवति मरै हुकमैं बूझै सोिए ।
नानक ऐसी मरनी जो मरै ता सद जीवण होिए ।
                                                बिहागडा की वार म: ४-सलोक म: ४
[182]घरमराइे है हरि का किआ हरिजन सेवक नेड़ ना आवैं ।
                                                      बिहागडे की वार म: ४
[183]जह साधू गोबिंद भजन..., निकटि न जाइओ दूत ।   गौड़ी म: ५
[184]नरकु सुरगु नही लबै लाग । मुकत बपुड़ी मी गिआनी तिआगैं ।   मारू म: १
[185]जह पैंडे महा अंध गुबारा । हरि का नामु संग उजीआरा ।   गौड़ी सुखमनी म: ५
[186]वालेवे कारणि बाबा रोिए रोवणु सगल बिकारो ।   वडहंस म: १

3

Sikh Religion

The Concept of Health

1. The Sikh Religion recognises the human body as the abode of God.[1] It is the temple of God, wherein the individual can see His Light. The human body is a microcosm wherein we can peep into the macrocosm and realize the Creator.[2] Like other temples the temple of human body has to be kept neat and clean with full veneration. It should be made a befitting house for the Lord. The cleanliness of mind and body takes the individual soul nearer God.[3] It has been well said by the wise people that cleanliness is godliness.

2. A healthy mind lives in a healthy body. The health of mind becomes the basis and cause of a healthy body. If mind is conquered, the whole world is conquered;[4] the body always remains fresh and glitters like gold.[5]

The extent of purity of mind makes the body flawless proportionately. Guru Arjan says, "That body is pure which does not commit sin."[6] Ordinarily, the night passes away in sleep and the day in eating, and in this manner the diamond-like body is wasted.[7] The human body is a rare phenomenon, we do not get it repeatedly like the ripe fruit of the forest, which when drops down, cannot be united with the bough.[8]

3. The gods are said to have a burning desire for the human body,[9] which is the only medium through which the soul reaches the desired goal. Out of the eighty-four lakhs of *yonis* the human being has been given this honour. The person who

slips down from this rung, experiences births, deaths and misery repeatedly.[10]

Therefore, when the body is without disease and old age and without the effect of death, the person should concentrate on the Lord.[11] All the other *yonis* are subservient to the human body,[12] which eats, drinks, plays, laughs and acts in several ways.[13] But as has been said above, the human body is obtained by the grace of the Lord,[14] therefore, it should be kept healthy for the highest type of actions (*karmas*).

4. In this vast universe, the Laws of God are seen working in all fields. The physical Law of Causation concerns the human body. Whenever, the poison is swallowed, it causes death.[15] Whenever some foreign material enters our body, it causes disease and if the disease is not checked properly, it causes the decay and death of the body. Proper diagnosis and suitable medicine can arrest the spread of the disease, therefore, the ideal doctor is expected to diagnose the type of illness and give the miracle medicine to the patient.[16] Guru Angad has addressed the Doctor in the following manner: "You can be a good Doctor, if firstly you diagnose the disease and secondly find out such cure as can remove many diseases. You can explore such a medicine, which can remove the disease and give comfort to the body. You can be a real doctor, if you remove your own illness."[17]

5. Whereas the Sikh Gurus talk of ego as the most dangerous disease,[18] they have clearly said that the worldly pleasures are the cause of the different types of diseases.[19] The body is filled with diseases of several kinds because of the sensual pleasures.[20] The five senses cause the illness in our body. The worldly enjoyments result in misery.[21] The more the enjoyments, the more the diseases.[22]

6. The Sikh Gurus have laid emphasis on continence (*Sanjam*).[23] Over-eating or gluttony is bad.[24] Under-nourishment is still worse. A balanced diet is necessary for the up-keep of health. A hungry person cannot be a healthy constituent of society. He cannot even think of God.[25] Guru Nanak has hit hard on the false proclamations of those who claim that they can live without eating cereals.[26] We cannot live without them. The *Gurus* have advised their followers to take a limited diet, which will keep both the body and mind quite fit.[27] We can

gain physical and mental health if we practise continence with regard to our senses of touch, sight, hearing, smell and taste.

7. We should eat such foods only, which do not tend to upset the physical and mental balance. Guru Nanak says, "Such foods (ought to be forbidden) which destroy our happiness, create pains in the body and bring up vices in the mind."[28] The Guru has not made any discrimination between a vegetarian and non-vegetarian diet. He says, "which is meat and which is grass? Who commits sin in eating them?"[29] His main concern is the moral and spiritual life. The Sikh Gurus have forbidden the use of intoxicants. One gains nothing but vices by using them.[30] Those who use the vicious drinks, destroy sanity and bring madness.[31] One loses hold on his senses, therefore, one should try to avoid these intoxicants to the farthest extent.[32]

8. For the unkeep of health, it is necessary to rise early in the morning.[33] Brushing of teeth[34] and taking a bath is compulsory.[35] One should not eat anything without taking bath.[36] Guru Arjan says, "Take a bath and remember the Lord. Your mind and body will become healthy."[37] Bhai Gurdas says, "I bow to those Sikhs of the Guru, who get up in the last hours of the night. I bow to those Sikhs of the Guru, who take bath in a tank in the early hours of the morning."[38] The Sikhs of the Guru eat less and sleep less.[39] They do not indulge in lust and anger[40] which are the cause of the destruction of the body.

9. The Sikh Religion is the religion of the householders, who are enjoined by their *Guru* to work and earn their living. A great emphasis has been laid on effort. One must work hard in order to not only support himself and his family, but also give tithe to the poor.[41]

One must do all the work with his hands and feet and keep his mind in tune with the Lord.[42] The work and effort on the part of the householders give sufficient exercise required for good health. Two more factors contribute towards the health of an individual:

  1. Keeping long hair; and
  2. Listening to or singing the divine music (*Hari-kirtan*).

The Sikhs wearing long hair have proved to be the best

warriors in the history of India (and even world). As regards *Hari-kirtan* (music) Guru Arjan says, "The person who listens to the divine music and sings it, does not experience any trouble."[43] The use of tobacco is strictly prohibited in Sikhism. The Sikhs do not smoke. It is a taboo for them.

The Concept of Yoga

The word Yoga means union

The *Yoga* system of Indian Philosophy is very old. Patanjali, the author of *Yoga Darshana* is said to be its founder. He adopted the *Sankhyan* philosophy, making an addition of Godhead. In his Yoga system, *yoga* does not mean the union of the individual self with God, but the cessation of all mental modifications (*cittavrittinirodha*). Several types of yoga have been mentioned in *Bhagavad Gita*, but emphasis has been laid on three types viz, *Karma yoga, Bhakti yoga* and *Gyan yoga*. In later times the concept of yoga deteriorated in the form of *Hath Yoga*, which emphasised the significance of nerves and nerve-centres in the human body.

Guru Nanak and the saint-poets preceding him had to face the yogis and especially the *Hath-yogis* of their times, who had established themselves and swayed the whole country with their miraculous feats. They had exploited the masses for their ends. Guru Nanak held several *Goshtas* (conversations) with them. One of such *Goshtas* namely *Siddh Goshta* has been included in the *Adi Granth*.

The beliefs and practices of contemporary yogis were not liked by Guru Nanak. He rejected outright all their formalism. He addresses them thus:

Yoga does not consist in wearing patched quilt, in carrying staff and in smearing the body with ashes.

Yoga does not consist in wearing ear-rings. In cutting hair and in playing on *Singhi* (musical instrument).

. . . *Yoga* does not consist in going to cremation ground and in abstract meditation,

Yoga does not consist in roaming about in the country and in bathing at holy places.[44]

Suhi, M. 1.

Then the question arises as to what is *yoga* and who is true *yogi*? Guru Nanak has given the answer to these questions in the same hymn and according to him the path of *yoga* consists in rising above all materialistic attachments while living in the world.[45] One who sees no difference in all *Jivas* is a *yogi*.[46] One can become a *yogi* by deed and not by word.[47] Guru Arjan considers the non-differential attitude as the sign of the path of *yogi*.[48] Guru Amar Das addresses the yogi in the following manner:

This is not *Yoga*, O *Yogi*:
If you leave your family and roam away.[49]

Ramkali Ashtpadi, M. III.

Thus the first requisite for *yoga* in Sikhism consists in leading a worldly or family life. In *Siddh Goshta* the *yogis* say:
He (the *yogi*) should remain away from towns and pathways
He should eat the wild fruit.
This is the wise saying of *Avdhut yogi*.[50]

But Guru Nanak rejects this path of the *yogis*. He clarifies his own point of view:

Just as the lotus remains unattached by water, the swan remains in the stream.
Similarly the disciple ought to meditate on the Word and cross the world-ocean by repeating the Name of the Lord.[51]

Herein the *Guru* has expounded the significance of *Surt-Shabad Yoga* or *Nam Yoga*. We may call the yoga of Guru Nanak by these names. The union with the Lord can be attained by the repetition of the Name of the Lord with utmost affection. The Name of the Lord becomes priceless for the disciple as the Lord Himself. This is the *Bhakti Yoga* of Guru Nanak. It has been named as *Sehj Yoga* by the great *Guru* in comparison to *Raja Yoga* of Patanjali and *Hath Yoga* of Gorakh Nath:

(1) The *Guru* with his union, subdued my mind which is always in *Bhakti Yoga*.

In the company of the *Guru* and saints all my ills have disappeared.

The union with *Hari* has been obtained in *Sehj*, saith

Nanak.[52]   *Basant*, M. I.

2. Make the Word of the *Guru* the ear-ring in your mind
 Use the quilt of modesty
 Whatever He does, accept it with resignation
 Obtain thus the treasure of *Sehj Yoga*.[53]   *Asa*, M. I.

Yoga is a discipline. Patanjali's *Yoga* consists of eight steps i.e. *yama* (self-restraint), *niyama* (observances), *pranayam* (regulation of breath), *Pratyahara* (withdrawing the senses), *Asan* (posture), *Dhyana* (contemplation), *Dharana* (fixation) and *Samadhi* (meditative trance). The positive and negative injunctions as expounded by *Yoga Darshana* are acceptable to Sikh Gurus. *Pranayam* and *Asanas* have been rejected. The *Gurus* have defined *Dhyana*, *Dharana* and *Samadhi* in their own way. In fact the stalwarts of *Bhakti* movement had their own concept of *Yoga*, but they used the already prevalent terminology in order to explain their own concept. The *Raja Yoga* of Guru Arjan is as follows:

The one Name be repeated with the tongue
It brings great happiness here and it has concern with the
   self in the next world.
The illness of ego vanishes
Thou mayst enjoy (this) *Raja Yoga* with the grace of the *Guru*
                                                             Gauri, M.V.[54]

This *Raja Yoga* is also called *Brahm Yoga* by Guru Ram Das in one of his hymns:

Brahm Yoga cannot be attained by guises
Hari can be realised through the company of the good.[55]
                                                                 Kanta, M. IV.

Raja Yoga can be attained by ending duality, by following the word of the *Guru*, by repeating the Name of the Lord, by singing His praises and by steadying the mind in all circumstances The *Yoga* of Sikh Gurus is a balanced union of all the three types of *Yoga* mentioned in *Gita* viz *Karma Yoga*, *Bhakti Yoga* and *Gyan Yoga*. The Sikh Gurus rejected the idea that one can realize Brahman through one of these *Yogas*. Action, devotion and knowledge—all are necessary for the union with Brahman.

The Concept of Bhakti

Bhakti or devotion takes its birth out of faith. For every individual, the first requisite of religious and devoted life is faith. A Muslim must have the prayer-mat of faith[56] and a *yogi*, the staff of faith.[57] Without faith there can be only deceit and no devotion.[58] Devotion demands complete self-surrender. The devotee cannot question the Will of the Lord.[59] Those who question, can never find a place in His Heart.[60] Therefore, the devotee must resign completely to the Will of the Lord. Fear of the Fearless Lord is a pre-requisite for devotion.[61] Ordinarily fear and love are two antagonistic factors in the development of human personality, but in the domain of devotion, they go side by side. The devotee is full of undefiled fear and pure love, fear of the omnipotent and love of the Merciful and Compassionate Lord.

The real devotion of *Hari* is His Love.[62] There are two types of devotion *i e. Loukika* and *Anuraga* or *Behranga* (outward) and *Antarang* (inward). The *Laukika devotion* is outward and formalistic and *Anuraga* devotion is inward. The Sikh **Gurus** have rejected the outward form of devotion. They have laid great emphasis on inward devotion *i.e.* pure love. Guru Amar Das has defined *Bhakti* in the following manner:

Whoever experiences inward love gets release
He controls his senses through the path of truth and
 continence.
He always remembers the Lord with the Word of the
 Guru.
This form of *Bhakti* is liked by *Hari*.[63]

Majh Ashtpadi, M. III.

The devotion which inspired a devotee to dance before the image of a god or goddess is rejected by the Sikh Gurus:
The fools practice devotion but exhibit themselves.
They dance and jump and are in great misery.
There can be no devotion by dancing and jumping
Whoever dies in Word, realises the true devotion.[64]

Gauri, M. III.

The devotee is loved by the Lord.[65] Guru Amar Das questions the birth of an individual without devotion, because he can never attain the Love and Grace of the Lord.[66]

There are nine types of *Bhakti* called *Naudha Bhakti* which include the devotion through 1. listening (*Sravan*) 2. music (*kirtan*), 3. Remembrance (*Simran*), 4. Washing the feet of the Lord (*Pad-Sevan*), 5. Service (*archan*) 6. bowing (*vandana*), 7. Obedience (*Das Bhav*), 8. Friendship (*Mitrata*) and self-surrender (*Atam Nivedan*). Suitable quotations regarding each type of *Bhakti* can be found out in the poetry of the Sikh Gurus, but prominence is given to *Prema Bhakti* or devotion through love. This path of devotion is very difficult to attain. It can only be attained through the graces of the Guru and Hari.[67] Guru Nanak is very emphatic on this point that there can be no devotion without the instruction of the Guru.[68]

When the disciple meets the *Guru* and receives instructions from him, the real devotion begins at that time. The devotee attains the holy nectar and crosses the world-ocean through his devotion of love.[69] Guru Arjan says:

O ignorant one! Receive the instruction of the Guru
Without devotion (*Bhakti*) many wise persons have perished.
O friend! Practise the devotion of *Hari* in your mind
Your *chit* (consciousness) will become pure.[70]

Gauri Sukhmani

Bhakti is the real path of *Nirvana*. The final emancipation can never be attained through learning and guises. The world is mad without *Bhakti*.[71] Without *Bhakti*, the human being looks like a dog or a swine.[72]

Bhakti is a type of *yoga* which unites a devotee with the Lord. Mention has already been made of *Bhakti Yoga*. Dhanna was a great devotee, who listened to the stories of earlier devotees *i.e.* Namdev, Kabir, Ravidas etc. and followed the path of love and ultimately realised his ideal. He became one with the Lord.[73]

The question arises about the path of devotion. How the devotee realises his objective? A true devotee questions himself:

Thou hast become free from attachment, defilement and sleep,
what grace hath befallen thee?
The most beautiful *maya* hath no influence on thee
where hath gone thy idleness?
Lust, anger and ego are very difficult to forsake

In what way thou hast released Thyself?
This *maya* hath looted all the worlds
 the god, man and demon have not escaped its three
            qualities,
This fire of *Avidya* (ignorance) hath burnt many a straw,
 some true disciple escapes it.
It is so powerful that I cannot express—
 I cannot express its praises.
But thou hast not become black in this mansion of antimony.
 Thou hast adopted pure colour.[74]   *Asa*, M.V.
The reply to the above questions comes in the succeeding verses:
The great *mantra* of the Guru resides in the heart
 thou hast listened to the queer Name
God hath showered his graces on thee
 and brought thee at His feet
The comfort hath been attained through the devotion
          of love, saith Nanak,
And mixing in the company of the good.[75]
            Asa, M.V.

The Word of the Guru is the treasure-house of devotion
Whoever sings, listens or practises it, attains his objective.[76]
The word of Guru inspires us to instil in our being the rare qualities, which form the basis of true devotion. One can never know these qualities and the practice of these qualities in his life without the aid of the true Guru and without these qualities there can be no devotion.[77] With these qualities, the Name of the Lord is instilled in our being and the union of the soul and Higher Soul is achieved.

The Concepts of Satguru and Name

In every walk of life we need a guide. In order to be proficient in a line, we have to get proper training. Similar is the case in the spiritual domain. For our spiritual uplift, we need a Guru or religious preceptor, who prepares us in thought,

THE CONCEPT OF SATGURU AND NAME

deed and action in order to make us a loving bride of the Lord. The Guru or *Satguru* is the kindly light, which sheds lustre on our path.

The institution of Guru is very old in India. In *Upanishads*, the last part of the *Vedas*, we find the Guru instructing his disciples. The disciple expresses his doubts and questions the seer, who gives apt replies, which are based on his personal experience. The Guru is the perfect being. He, who has realised Brahman, may be called *Satguru*.[78] But there have been innumerable pretenders in every age, who deceived their disciples and had only their material gains in view. They danced before their disciples in several guises for the sake of their bread.[79] The Sikh Gurus and the Saint-poets of the *Adi Granth* have painted these pretenders in their true colours. A blind preceptor always drowns his companions.[80] If the master is naked and hungry, how can his servant have to his fill?[81]

In the *Adi Granth*, nearly every hymn talks directly or indirectly about the Guru. The Guru is the pivot of the whole Sikh thought. The abundance of the praises of the Guru misled Dr. Trumpp when he said, "The high position, which the Guru claimed for himself, naturally led to *deification* of the same, and though Nanak spoke of himself and confessed himself unlearned and the lowest of sinners, the following Gurus soon commenced, owing to the abject flattery of their adherents, to identify the Guru with the Supreme Himself. The consequence was such a deification of man as has hardly ever been heard of elsewhere. Life, property and honour were sacrificed to the Guru in a way, which is often revolting to our moral feelings. It was therefore a very fortunate event for the more free and moral development of the Sikh community, that with the tenth Guru Gobind Singh, the Guru-ship was altogether abolished."* This view of Dr. Trumpp is the result of his ignorance of the Indian thought and tradition. The reverence for the Guru is not only delineated in Sikhism, it is also found in *Upanishads*, *Tantras* and *Agamas*. For the disciple his Guru is *Brahma*, *Vishnu* and *Shiva*.[82] For the disciple his Guru is a vast ocean, a holy place of pilgrimage, a

---

*The *Adi-Granth* or the Holy Scripture of the Sikhs by Dr. Ernest Trumpp, (ed. 1877) Chapter, Sketch of the Religion of the Sikhs, cx-cxi.

ship, a sailor, a philosopher's stone, a moneylender, a jeweller, a guide, a mahout, a doctor, a warrior, a mediator etc.[83] He looks at his preceptor from different angles.

But the question arises about the physical aspect of the Guru-Soul. In the primal age, the Guru-Soul was identical with Brahman. This shows that the first and the foremost Guru is God Himself. Guru Nanak and Guru Gobind Singh talk of Him as their Guru.[84] When the universe was created by Brahman, the Guru-Soul pervaded the universe as *Ishvara*, but when *Ishvara* became manifest through an enlightened Soul in a physical form, it adopted several names in different times. These enlightened souls through whom the Word of God or Name spread in the universe were called Gurus. The ten Gurus of the Sikhs are the ten manifestations of the Guru-Soul. All the contributors of the *Adi Granth* experienced the manifestation of the Guru-Soul within them. Since this scripture contains the message of the Guru-Soul, his Word or *Bani*, it was given the status of a Guru by Guru Gobind Singh. The physical form disappeared with the tenth Guru and the Guru-Soul manifested itself in the form of Word, Name or *Bani*. In fact, the body is prone to death, but the Word lives on for ever. In the *Adi Granth*, the significance of *Guru Bani* or Word has been depicted in the following manner:

1. The *Bani* is Guru, Guru is the *Bani* and all the ambrosias exist in *Bani*.   *Nat Ashtpadi*, M. IV.
   If the disciple follows the saying of Vani, the Guru takes the disciple across the world-ocean.[85]
2. The Word is the Guru and the concentration is the disciple[86]   *Ramkali*, M.I

When the *Guru* is in the physical form, he possesses the following attributes:

1. He has realised Brahman.[87]
2. He is anxious to get the release of all humanity. He is merciful. He forgives the sinners.[88]
3. He is the field of piety.[89]
4. He is without enmity. He sees Brahman all around. Everybody is equal in his eyes.[90]
5. He is the giver of comfort and the destroyer of evils.[91]
6. Whoever meets him, finds bliss.[92]

THE CONCEPTS OF *SATGURU* AND NAME

7. He is like Himalayas.[93]
8. He gives the knowledge of Brahman.[94]
9. He gives Name or Word to the disciple.[95]
10. For his disciple he is like father, mother, master, God, friend, relative and brother.[96]
11. He is the key bearer of the House of the Lord. Only He can open it.[97]

The two significant functions of the Guru are:
1. imparting *Guru mantra* or Word or the Name of the Lord to the disciple.
2. imparting the knowledge of Brahman.

The *mantra* or the word of the Guru is Guru himself, therefore, the greatest service of the Guru consists in the repetition of this *mantra* with faith and love. Just as the water is contained in the pitcher and without water there can be no pitcher, in a similar manner the mind is controlled by the knowledge and there can be no knowledge without the Guru.[98] The Word of the Guru destroys ego and the knowledge imparted by the *Guru* destroys the poisonous fangs of maya, the she-serpent Guru Arjan says:

> I have broken off from the deceitful she-serpent.
> The Guru told me that she was false and fraudulent.
> She is a bitter pill coated with sugar.
> But my mind is satisfied with the nectar of Name.
> I have broken off from the company of greed and attachments
> The merciful Guru hath given me refuge.
> This trickish (*maya*) hath ruined many a house.
> We have been saved by the merciful Guru.
> I have broken off from lust and anger
> I have heard the instruction of the Guru with my own ears.
> Whenever I see, the supreme demon is there
> We have been saved by the Guru and God.
> The senses and sense-organs have been made widows by me.
> The Guru told me that they were like poisonous fire
> Whoever hath any concern with them goes to hell
> We have been saved by the *Guru* through love of God.
> I have broken off from ego
> The Guru told me that it was foolish and obstinate
> It is homeless, it can never find a home

We have been saved by the Guru through love of God
We have become inimical to these people
Both cannot live in the same house
We have come to the Lord and taken refuge in Him.
Do justice, O Omniscient Lord!
God spoke with us smilingly and did justice
He put in my service all the servants
Thou art my master, all this house is Thine.
The Guru hath given his decision, saith Nanak.[99]

Prabhati Ashtpadi, M.V.

The above verses make it clear that in the company of the Guru, the five principal evils dwindle away and we realise the Lord. The miracle is brought about by the *mantra* imparted by the Guru, therefore, the real Guru is this *mantra* and the promulgator of *mantra* is none else than the first Lord. The human teacher is a representative of the Divine. In other words he may be called the Divine itself in human form.

The *Tantras* have also taken a similar view about the Guru. In the *Yogini Tantra* it is written:

"He who is the first Lord and is called *Mahakal* is the Guru, *O Devi!* in all *Mantras*. None else is the Guru. He is verily the Guru of the Shaivas, Shaktas, Vaishnavas, Ganapatyas, Moon-worshippers, Mahashaivas and Sauras. He and none else is the promulgator of *Mantra*. *At the time of imparting Mantra*, O daughter of mountain! *He manifests Himself in him who imparts mantra*. Hence *O Devi!* verily there is no Guruship in man.... Because He manifests Himself in the human Guru, therefore, the greatness of the human Guru is published in all the Shastras."*

In *Vishvasara Tantra* the following significant words occur about the Guru: "The appearance of the Guru is the root of *Dhyana*, the lotus-foot of the Guru is the foot of *Puja*, the Word of the Guru is the root of *Mantra* and the grace of the Guru is the root of *Siddhi*."†

Guru Arjan has depicted and classified the above ideas about the Guru in one of his hymns:

Bring the appearance (*murti*) of the Guru in the
Dhyana of the mind.

*Quoted from *Studies in the Tantras and the Veda* by M. P. Pandit.
†ibid.

THE CONCEPTS OF *SATGURU* AND NAME

Accept the word of the Guru as the *mantra* in your mind,
Adopt the feet of the Guru in your heart
Always bow before the Guru—the Higher Brahman.
None in the world should remain in doubt
No body can cross the world-ocean without the Guru.
The *Guru* has put me on the right path
I have broken off from everything except devotion.
The fear of transmigration has been removed.
This is the infinite greatness of the perfect Guru.
With the Grace of the Guru, the downward lotus hath
                                        blossomed up.
The light hath spread in the darkness.
The Creator hath been realised by me through the Guru.
With the grace of the Guru, the foolish mind hath come on
                                        the right path.
The Guru is the Creator. He hath power to do everything
The Guru is the Supreme *Ishvara*, Who is and will be.
God hath taught me this, saith Nanak.
We cannot achieve final emancipation without the Guru.[106]
                                                    Gaund, M.V.

    The True Guru includes the functions of both of *Shiksha* Guru (teaching *Guru*) and the *Diksha* Guru (initiating Guru), These functions are the imparting of knowledge of the path and the initiation. The initiation is done through a *Mantra* or the *Word*. The Guru guides the disciple at every step and *Siddhi* is attained only through his guidance.

    A *mantra* which may be called sacred syllable or Word is an invocation to the Deity. The *mantra* occurs in two forms. One form is the regular prayer in words. In this respect many hymns of the *Adi Granth* may be called *mantras*. The practice of *mantras* for the fulfilment of worldly desires has been rejected by the Sikh Gurus as mere incantations and charms. Only such mantra or mantras are acceptable, as are imparted by the true Guru for the sake of the union of the disciple with the Lord. The *Mul-mantra* is the significant *mantra* in Sikhism, which occurs in the very beginning of the *Adi Granth*. The other form of *mantra* is the combination of syllables. It may be called *Bija-mantra*[101] (seed *mantra*), Word of the Guru or the Name of the Lord. Since Guru is a field of piety, the seed *mantra* from that field can only grow in the disciple-field wit a simihlar climate and similar efforts. The syllables o *bija*-mantra inf Sikhism *i.e. Wahuguru* are the sound bodies of Brahman. They reproduce in human speech the original sound-vibrations that accompany the manifestation of *Ishvara*. When repeated, these sounds act as evocations to *Ishvara* and provide the body *Ishvara* fotor manifestation to the aspiring devotee. In the *Bija-mantra* of the Sikhs *i.e. Wahu Guru* the word Guru is for *Para Brahman* and *Wahu* the combination of *Wa* and *ha* fstand or the wonderful. The combination of *Wa* and *ha* also occurs in the tenth section of *Taittiriya Upanishad* as *ha vu ha vu ha vu* which means 'oh wonderful, oh wonderful, oh wonderful.' The sound-bodies of *Waha Guru* manifest before the disciple 'the wonderful *Para Brahman.* Brahman may be called by countless names by the disciples, who create these names according to the attributes of their Godhead, but the real name of God is '*Sat,*' which is the first and the foremost. It shows Brahman as ever-existent.

Since the *Word* of the Guru is *Bija-mantra* or the Name of the Lord, it grows into the heart of devotee as *Ishvara*, therefore, the seed-*mantra* is sometimes called Brahman or *Shabad Brahm.*

None of the meritorious works equals the Name of the Lord.[102] All the sins are washed away with it.[103] Those who repeat or listen to it become pure.[104] They attain bliss. The Name of Hari is like *Parjat* and *Kamadhena*.[105] It fulfils all the wishes of the devotee. The best religion of all is the Name of Hari, the remembrance of which is the best action.[106] It preserves us in all conditions and finishes all our hungers and desires.[107] Through it we attain the peace of mind.[108] The whole world is diseased and the Name of the Lord is the only remedy. The disease occurs in the absence of Truth.[109]

Early hours of the morning known as *Amrit-vela* (the time for the receipt of the Nectar) is the best time for concentration, therefore, it is the best time for the remembrance of the Name of the Lord.[110] But there is no bar regarding the other parts of the day for the purpose. The true devotee remembers the Lord in all his actions and postures *i.e.* standing, sleeping or walking.[111] One may be at home or in journey, the whole hearted remembrance at all times under the guidance of the

Guru fulfils our objective.[112] The advice of Namdev to Trilochan must be followed by every disciple. "Do all the work with your hands and feet but keep your *chit* or conscious factor in tune with the Lord."[113] But the question arises—How can we remember the Lord in our sleep? The sleep is only meant for the tired body. The body may take rest, but the soul is always awake. The body may relax but the mind is always on the move. This mind, which is an outer covering of the soul along with *buddhi* (intellect) has to be trained on the right path, so that the soul becomes conscious of its entity. In this way, we can always (even in sleep) remain in tune with Infinite. Kabir says: if a person repeats the Name of the Lord in his dream, I am ready to cast off my body for his shoes.[114]

Some people argue and question the utility of the Name of the Lord. The devotee, who is always imbued with the Name, subdues his ego and kills his evil thoughts by his whole-time engagement with the Name. He performs all his worldly duties, but he never swerves from the right path, always working under the instruction and guidance of the Guru. The outer and inner disorders fill our houses with dirt every day and the housewife sweeps it regularly, similarly the Name regularly sweeps away the dirt of ego *etc*. from our minds and makes us worthy devotees of the Lord. The Name and ego cannot live at one plane.[115] Several maunds of fuel is consumed with a spark of fire, similarly the great number of sins are consumed by the devotional remembrance of the Name.[116] The Name saves us from the dreadful *yama*. It helps us at the time of death as a true friend. It helps us in all difficulties, at all times. The Lord himself appears and takes his devotee out of all the difficulties and troubles.

The person who is imbued with the Name of the Lord has the following attributes:

He is a warrior with perfect forbearance
    and intelligence.
He is in *Sehj* meditation, deep and serene.
He is ever released and his works are complete.
In whose heart resides the Name of *Hari*,
He has all comforts, he is blissful and healthy.
All are equal in his eyes. He is perfectly unattached
He neither comes nor goes and never swerves,

In whose mind the Name of the Lord resides.[117]

Ramkali, M.V.

All the works and actions enjoined by Shastras for the emancipation remain far inferior to the remembrance of the Name of the Lord. The significance of the Name has been very well propounded in *Sukhamani* by Guru Arjan Dev. Without the Name of the Lord, a human being wastes his life[118] and can never attain the peace of mind. The world is like fire and the Name of the Lord is like cold water.[119]

Now the question arises as to how a disciple has to traverse the path of *Nam-Yoga*. The first and common method of the remembrance of the Name is through the tongue, about which Guru Nanak says in *Japji*:

If a tongue multiplies into a lakh and it grows into twenty lakhs,
And if we repeat the Name of the Lord a lakh times with a tongue,
In this way we can climb the rungs of reverence and become one with the Lord.[120]

But the Gurus have laid emphasis on the practice and not only on speech. Whoever practises in the mind and through the mouth recites the Name of *Hari*, that person does not swerve in this or the next world.[121] People may repeat the Name of the Lord through their tongues, but that will never bring the peace of mind. If the Name resides in the heart through the grace of the Guru, the devotee will get the desired result.[122] All repeat the Name of Hari with their mouths, but the person in whose heart the Name resides is a rarity.[123] The final emancipation can only be obtained, when the Name resides in the heart. The remembrance of the Name can bring no fruit, if the life of a person is corrupt.[124]

The second method of the remembrance of the Name of the Lord is through breath. Each breath going inward and outward bears the Name. In this way a time comes, when the remembrance becomes spontaneous. The repetition of the Name continues through breath in every walk of life. The tongue does not work in this case and only the mind works with the breath.

Without tongue who repeats with the breath the Name of the Lord, he is rarity.[125]

Malar, M. 1.

This method may not be mistaken for *Pranayam* of the yogis. *Pranayam* requires a complicated practice of the regulation of breath, but the method of the Guru is quite simple. Just as the beads are put together in a rosary by the aid of a thread, in a similar manner the thread of the breath combines together the beads of the Name of the Lord. This method may bring in more concentration, but it may be a hasty and slippery step. The first method can be utilised by common people and the second by more refined ones.

In the more mature stages, when the devotee can think of nothing else except the Name of the Lord, the Name is uttered through every pore of the body.[126] The advanced stage of the remembrance of the Name is known as *Ajapa Jap i.e.* the spontaneous remembrance.

The Concepts of Sadh Sangat and Kirtan

Whereas a True Sikh is a member of an ideal society, he is also a member of an ideal company. This ideal company may be called *Sadh Sangat*, the company of the saints or the company of the good. An ideal company may be called a miniature ideal society. But the word 'society' has a much wider significance. A company is a small group working within that society. This group may be quite at variance in morals and manners than the rest of the groups in the same society.

The ideal company is a group of persons, some of whom are true Sikhs and some may be trying to become true disciples. and other may be mere novices. But when this company gathers together, the spirit of the true Guru resides in it, because it concentrates only on the Name of the Lord.[127] It is a privilege to secure a seat in this company, because the true Name becomes the sustenance of the mind[128]

In a strict sense, the general meetings or *Dewans*, where the motive of the visit of many is not the concentration on the Name, cannot be called *Sadh Sangat* or *Sat Sang*. In the company of the good the mind becomes pure.[129] It considers itself as the dust of the feet of everybody; every one is its friend.[130] The company of saints is considered extremely pure, the touch of which creates the love of the Lord. With the maturity of this love, one attains the state of bliss and crosses the world-ocean.[131]

Guru Arjan Dev has delineated the significance of *Sadh Sangat* in the following verses:

> The crippled may cross a mountain
> The fool may make wise speech
> The blind may see the three worlds having become pure on meeting the *Guru*
> O my friend, listen, the praises of *Sadh Sangat*
> The dirt is cast off, millions of sins are gone,
> The *Chit* becomes pure
> The cat hath become a lion, the straw seems like a mountain
> Those who worked hard for a penny have become very rich.[132]
>
> Bilawal, M.V.

The company of the good is like a philosopher's stone, which turns ordinary people into gold.[133] The member of this company falls in love with the Name of the Lord and realises Truth.[134] This company is like a boat, which takes the inmate beyond this world-ocean and who is never born again.[135] The pure intellect dawns upon him and his overturned mind-lotus blossoms. He is cool, calm and content.[136] All his desires are extinguished. The mind does not run in different directions and the pure abode is achieved.[137]

When the sinner enters this company of the good, he is not discarded but graciously initiated into the discipline. He absorbs gradually the fragrance of *Sadh Sangat* like an ordinary plant near the sandal-wood taking its qualities. In the company of the good, the novice gets the instructions of the Guru. In this case, the *Sangat* becomes the Guru. As has been told above, the spirit of the Guru resides in the *Sangat*. Any talk or conversation or speech within the *Sangat* is about the Name of the Lord and the disciple who belongs to this company becomes a saint and rises above duality.

Guru Arjan has dealt at length about the company of the *Saints* and *Sadhs* in his longer poem *Sukhmani*. These saints are the cream of the society, whose touch melts the hardest of

THE CONCEPTS OF SADH SANGAT AND KIRTAN

hearts.[138] Whoever comes in their contact, forgets all jealousies.[139] He is the friend of all and has no enemy.[140] In the company of the best men, one becomes like them; he casts off all the evils, while taking in all the qualities.[141] The words *Sant, Sat* or *Sadh* attached with *Sangat* (*i.e.* company) lay emphasis on its saintliness, truthfulness and discipline. *Sat Sangat* is a school of True Guru, where the disciple learns about the qualities of Hari, which he has to imbibe within himself.[142]

In the *Shlokas* of Kabir, we find much about the company of the good, Some examples are given below:

1. Kabir says: Such is the bad result of a bad company.
   Just as a thorny Ber tree near a Banana tree
   The one dangles about and the other is torn.
   Do not seek the company of the *Shaktas*.[143]
2. Kabir says: The Sandal-tree is good.
   It is surrounded by Dhak and Palas trees.
   Those which dwell near the sandal-tree become sandal themselves.[144]
3. Kabir says: Do not follow the example of Bamboo, which is egoistic of its greatness.
   Though it dwells near the sandal-tree, it does not become fragrant.[145]
4. The saint does not cast away his saintliness.
   Though he comes across millions of wicked people
   The sandal-tree does not give up its coolness
   Though it is surrounded by snakes.[146]

The abode, where the *Sadh Sangat* congregates, is known as *Gurdwara* or the house of the Guru. After the passing away of the tenth Guru, the Guruship passed on to *Granth Sahib*. Thus every *Gurdwara* is the abode of *Guru Granth Sahib* and the *Sadh Sangat* is presided over by the Guru through its *Bani*. After every prayer in the *Gurdwara*, the following verses are repeated daily:

The Panth was started by the order of the Timeless.
And Sikhs are ordained to accept *Granth Sahib* as their **Guru**.
Granth Sahib may be accepted as the manifestation of the Guru.
Whoever hath a pure heart, can find the Guru in the WORD.[147]

The disciples gathered together in a congregation belong to

different spiritual status according to their efforts and the Grace of the Guru. The indwelling Guru helps them and each one of them helps his fellow disciple up to the extent of his own experience in the spiritual domain. The words of the Guru or *Guru Bani* guide the disciples at every step.

The main function of *Sadh Sangat* is the remembrance of the Name of the Lord. For this purpose, each disciple concentrates on the Word and the music of the sweet songs of the Guru not only helps him to drink deep the nectar of *vani*, but also helps him in further spiritual flights. The singing of *Guru Bani* is known as *Kirtan*. The word *Kirtan* literally means the singing of the praises of the Lord, therefore, literally *Kirtan* is divine music.

Music or *Kirtan* is like invaluable diamond, full of bliss and deep in qualities.[148] Whoever listens or sings the *Kirtan* of Hari, no trouble can come near him. Plato also gives a similar idea. According to Plato music is valuable not only because it brings refinement of feeling and character, but also because it preserves and restores health. He says further that music and measure lend grace and health to the soul and to the body.

A disciple who concentrates on the feet of the Lord, keeping in mind His Name and who performs *Kirtan* in the company of the Saints, the messengers of *Yama* keep away from him.[149] *Kirtan* is significant mode of devotion (*Bhakti*); it brings bliss and comfort to the devotee.[150] The kingdom and the material gains are of no worth. If *Kirtan* of Hari is the sustenance, this is the permanent wealth.[151] Whoever performs the *Kirtan* of Hari or listens to His praises is loved by the Lord Himself.[152]

The disciple who listens to the *Kirtan* of *Hari* casts off enmity and jealousy from his mind.[153] A devotee, who always performs the *Kirtan* and remembers the Name, never faces any trouble.[154] On whomsoever the Lord showers his graces, the *Kirtan* of Hari becomes his sustenance.[155] His mind is always awake in the *Kirtan* of Hari, which removes all his dirt of ego.[156]

Guru Arjan Dev gives the following advice to the devotee:
If you require permanent bliss, O brother!
The *Guru* has told us to go in the company of the saint,
Where one remembers only the Name of the Lord.
In this company we cross the world-ocean.

Of all elements the most significant is the element of
knowledge.
Of all meditations the most significant is the meditation
of ONE.
Of all sounds the most significant is the *Kirtan of Hari*.
When the devotee meets the *Guru*, he sings the praises of the
Lord, saith Nanak.[157] *Basant*, M. V.

Guru Arjan further enjoins the devotee to sing the *Kirtan* of *Hari* day and night. This is the only fruitful work.[158] The prayer of a devotee to the Lord should be for the bestowal of strength to sing His praises.[159] It will not be out of place here to mention that although Guru Nanak practically demonstrated his love for *Kirtan* by always keeping the bard *Mardana* with him, Guru Arjan brought the *Kirtan* from a particular section of society to the company of the true Sikhs or *Sadh Sangat*. Every Sikh or Sangat needed this food of divine love.

The Concepts of a True Sikh and an Ideal Society

The ideal Society envisaged by the Sikh Gurus is not Utopia, but a reality which may bring in *Kritayuga* within *Kaliyuga*. The Concept of Guru Nanak about the Society matured in the form of *Khalsa* in the time of Guru Gobind Singh. The Khalsa is a universal brotherhood, voicing the concept of 'One World.' It demolishes all the walls of prejudices between man and man, man and woman, religion and religion, the rich and poor, king and his subjects. It breaks away all the shackles of formalism; it gives freedom about food, shelter and clothing.

The Sikh brotherhood is free from any distinction of caste. No Sikh considers himself superior to any other. Humility and modesty are his specialities, therefore, the service of humanity is the main aim of his life. Every individual of Sikh Society is a saint, soldier and scholar, therefore, the society itself is martial in spirit, saintly in character and scholarly in knowledge.

Guru Gobind Singh himself writes about the *Khalsa* in the following manner:
   Who remembers the ever-awakening light day and night
   Who doth not bring in his mind other than ONE
   Who is faithful and full of pure love
   Who hath no faith in *Vratas* (fasts), graves, temples at all
   Who does not recognise anything except ONE
   Even forsakes the holy places, charity, mercy, austerity and
      continence
   In whose heart is enlightened the perfect light
   Then He is *Khalsa*-then he be known as Pure.[160]
                                              Swayya, No. 1

An ideal society is group of those individuals who have full satisfaction about their day-to-day requirements. Unless their requirements are fulfilled, there can be no peace of mind and an individual cannot think of God or His devotion. Kabir is very emphatic on this point:
   There can be no devotion while I am hungry
   You can take away this rosary.
   I beg for the dust of the feet of the saints
   I am not indebted to anybody
   O *Madhva*! How can I become yours?
   If you will not care for me, I shall beg of Thee
   I ask for two seers of flour
   A quarter seer of *Ghee* with some salt
   I ask for half a seer of pulse
   So that I may be able to live for the day.
   I ask for a four-legged cot,
   With a pillow and a bed
   And a quilt to take over,
   Then I can devote myself to Thee with full zeal.
   I have not asked for anything out of greed
   I am a great lover of Thy Name
   My mind hath gone with Thee, saith Kabir,
   When the mind submits, God is realized.[161]   *Sorath Kabir*

Another saint Dhanna sings in the same strain:
   O *Gopal*, I perform thine *aarti*
   Whoever is devoted to Thee, all his wishes are fulfilled.

THE CONCEPTS OF A TRUE SIKH AND AN IDEAL SOCIETY

> I ask for pulse, flour and *ghee*
> Which may always please my mind.
> Good clothes and shoes I ask
> And corn from a well-ploughed land
> I ask for a milching cow and a buffalo
> And a good mare to ride upon.
> A faithful wife—
> Thy servant Dhanna asks for this.[162]

The above examples show that a satisfied individual can think of devotion or love of God. Indian thinkers and seers have talked of four requirements of life *viz. Dharma* (piety), *Artha* (material gains), *Kama* (fulfilment of worldly desires) and *Moksha* (final emancipation). In an ideal society, all these four requirements are fulfilled. But the modern world only thinks of *Artha* and *Kama* and neglects the other two. *Dharma* is an essential requisite which brings maturity for *moksha*, but a balanced activity in the field of *Artha* and *Kama* is necessary.

The Sikh religion is a religion of activity, therefore, it enjoins every individual to lead the life of a householder. It rejects *varnas* and *ashramas* and lays emphasis on equality and fraternity. Every individual has to plunge into the field of action; his path is *pravritti marga*. While following this path, he has to remain under a discipline ordained by the preceptor. We have already talked about this discipline in the chapter on "The concept of virtue and vice." While remaining in this world of activity, the individual earns for himself and his family and is even in a position to give *tithe* (*daswandh*) for the good of others. With the attainment of *artha* his *kama* is fulfilled and following the path of *piety* (*Dharma*) he gradually matures himself under the guidance of the preceptor for his real destination *i.e. Moksha*.

But the responsibility of the welfare of the society rests on the shoulders of the State. The State has to take the responsibility of the provision of food, shelter and clothing to every individual of the society. Every individual must be provided with work according to his aptitude. Kabir was a weaver and Namdev was a calico printer. Work is essential for every individual. Work is worship. The sincere worker is a *yogi*. He can never think of evil and can traverse the path of piety with great facility and ease. Man performs the outdoor duties and the woman has great domestic responsibilities. All the components of society have to work jointly for the common good also. The prayer of the individual of an ideal society is "the good of all under the Will of the Lord."[163]

The king or the chief of State should be an ideal personality in whom all his subjects can respose confidence. He should be humble servant of the poor. He should follow the democratic principles, without which his kingdom is sure to fall after some time.[164] He should be worthy of the throne and his officials should be God-fearing and law-abiding persons. The king and his officials should only take from the subjects whatever is reasonable,[165] and with which they can reasonably manage the affairs of the State.

Woman is the most significant part of the society, who gives birth to the greatest individuals of the society.[166] She should receive the utmost reverence. She is not only the better-half, she is also a gate for emancipation.[167] As a daughter, sister, mother and wife she should receive the due respect. She has equal rights in the society. The Sikh Gurus believed like Plato that there is to be no sex-barrier of any kind in the community, not even in education; the girl should have the same intellectual opportunities as the boy. Why a widow should not be allowed to re-marry? Why a woman be burnt to ashes with the dead? Guru Amar Das spoke severely against the custom of 'Sati.'[168] The woman has the same soul as the man and she has an equal right to grow spiritually, equal right to attend religious congregations and recite divine hymns in the temples.

For a father the daughter is not inauspicious and it is the duty of the parent to give her proper training. For a brother the sister is a sacred trust. He has to swear to save the honour of the sister under all circumstances. For a husband his wife is better-half. Throughout his life he has to remain faithful to her. Polygamy is a sin. 'One man and one wife' is the golden principle.[169] Whatever is said about a man, the same can be said about a woman. She has to remain faithful to her husband throughout his life.

It is the duty of the State to better the lot of poor people in society. Any case of harshness towards the poor leads one farther from God. They are punished in the court of the

THE CONCEPTS OF A TRUE SIKH AND AN IDEAL SOCIETY

Lord.[170] In an ideal society, no question of poverty arises. Every individual gets his due.

An individual in an ideal society must be great physically, mentally and spiritually. A member of such a Sikh society must be a 'Model Man' or a True Sikh. The term "True Sikh" does not confine itself only to a male Sikh; the female is equally represented. In the terminology of the *Adi Granth*, a True Sikh is called "Gurmukh"—one who strictly follows the instructions of the True *Guru*.

Guru Ram Das has defined the True Sikh in the following manner:

> Whoever calls himself a Sikh of the True Guru,
> He gets up in the early hours of the morning and remembers the Name of the Lord.
> He puts in great effort to get up before dawn and take a bath in the tank of nectar.
> Under the instructions of the *Guru* he recites the Name of *Har*
> And in this way he sheds *off* all his sins.
> Then, when the day dawns, He sings the *bani* of the *Guru*.
> And remembers the Name of the Lord, while sitting and standing.
> He who remembers my Lord with every breath and loaf, that Sikh is loved by the *Guru*.
> On whom my Lord showers His Grace,
> The *Guru* gives instructions to that Sikh.
> I ask for the dust of the feet of that Sikh of the *Guru*,
> Who recites himself and makes others recite the Name of the Lord.[171]

The true Sikh may be called a *Gurmukh, Sant, Sadh, Jivan mukta* or *Brahm Giani*, because under the instructions of the Guru he becomes an adept, a saint, a *Sadh* or realiser of Brahman while being alive. The attributes of a *Sant, Sadh* and *Brahm Giani* have been fully dealt with in *Sukhmani* of Guru Arjan and that of a *Gurmukh* in several poems including *Siddh Goshta* of Guru Nanak and the *Vars* of Bhai Gurdas. A Sikh remains a Sikh but whenever the Lord or the Primal Guru wants, he can attain the position of *Satguru*. This happened in the case of Guru Angad, Guru Amar Das, Guru Ram Das, Guru Arjan Dev, Guru Hargobind *etc*.

A true Sikh is an ideal man, who can be a proper component

of an ideal society. He is ethically and spiritually great. The following two quotations will give a true picture about him:

1. The disciple (*Gurmukh*) recites the Name of the Lord,
    gives charity to the deserving and takes bath (in the tank of nectar).
   The disciple attains full concentration in *Sehj*
   The disciple receives respect in the court of the Lord
   The disciple destroys all fear and is (really) great
   The disciple acts supremely and makes others act like that
   The disciple meets the Lord and helps others to meet Him,
       saith Nanak.[172]   *Siddh Goshta*

2. The disciple (*Gurmukh*) speaks sweetly
    Whatever he speaks, it is the recitation of the Name
   The disciple sees with his eyes
    but his sight is the concentration of his self on Brahman
   The disciple hears attentively
    but he hears the word of the Guru, which is *Panch Shaba* for him.
   The disciple works
    and the work is his obeisance to the Lord
   The disciple follows the path
    and he deems it an honour to circumambulate it.
   The disciple eats and wears
    and this is a yoga for him.
   The disciple sleeps in abstract meditation
   The disciple is a house-holder, without any extraneous help
    he is *a jivanmukta*.
   he is un-influenced by the ripples of greed.
   He is above boon and curse.[173]

                              Var, 6. Pauri 18, Bhai Gurdas

The Sikh Ceremonies

The Sikh Gurus have rejected the performance of all kinds of works which result in ego and duality. For them all those actions are commendable which help us in the realization of

our ultimate objective *i.e.* the union with the Lord. Guru
Arjan says:
> All the other works are useless except those about Hari.[174]
>   *Gauri*, M.V.

The *Nitya* and *Naimittika* Karmas enjoined by Hindu
Shastras have not been given any place in *Sikh Ethics*. The
good works on which emphasis has been laid by the *Adi
Granth* are the cultivation of moral qualities which form the
basis of spiritual development. These Karmas may be called
Higher Karmas.

In a sense, there are no rituals and formal ceremonies which
must be performed by a Sikh. A Sikh is a saint and a saint
has nothing else to do except to adore his Guru and to follow
his instructions. His primary function is the remembrance of
the Name of the Lord, which he has received from his
preceptor. He has not to go to any other *Sadh* except his
Guru. His Guru is *Granth Sahib* and the abode of his Guru is
Gurdwara. But a Sikh is also a house-holder. The male has to
earn the bread for the family and the female has to look after
the upkeep of the house and the welfare of the family.

Thus a Sikh has twin duties to perform, the secular as well
as divine. But these secular duties very often verge on the
divine border, because in every work the Sikh seeks the divine
grace.

The Nitya Karmas of a Sikh

The daily life of a Sikh can be described in the following way:
1. He has to get up at about 4.00 A.M. in the morning.
   This time is considered best for concentration.
   There are several verses in[175] the *Adi Granth* which
   pointedly enjoin a Sikh to get up before dawn
   (*Amritvela*), when a true Sikh can savour the divine nectar.
2. He must take a bath. Natural or cold water is
   recommended for this. Warm water, however, can be
   used, in the case of ill-health.
3. After cleansing and clothing all parts of the body, he
   has to concentrate himself on the Divine Lord with his
   prayer. His prayer consists of some portions of
   Nitnem. *Japji*, the famous poem of Guru Nanak is
   recited at this time. This poem is also called the

morning prayer. Jap Sahib and ten *Swayyas* of Guru Gobind Singh are also recited at this time. He may also repeat the Name of the Lord on which he can concentrate at all times.

4. After his *Nitnem*, he must go to a *Gurdwara*, the abode of the Guru for his *darshan* and instructions. The assembly of the Sikhs in the *Gurdwara* is *Sadh Sangat* or the holy congregation, which is considered very useful for the spiritual development. The Guru is said to manifest himself through the *Sangat*. In a *Gurdwara* the priest opens the holy scripture *Guru Granth Sahib* in the morning on a raised platform and under a canopy. In the presence of his scripture the Sikh feels the presence of the Guru, because his scripture is his Guru. The holy book is opened in the beginning of the day and closed late in the evening after evening prayers. On both these occasions, a hymn from the holy *Granth* is read out.

5. In the *Sadh Sangat* the Sikh attentively listens to the *bani* of the Guru in the form of recitation either directly from *Guru Granth Sanib* or in the form of *Kirtan* (Divine Music), when the hymns of Gurus are sung. *Asa ki var*, a longer poem of Guru Nanak is recited every day through *Kirtan* in *Raga Asa*.

6. The *Anand Sahib*, a longer poem of Guru Amar Das brings the daily congregational functions to a close. The shloka at the end of *Japji* is also recited at this time.

7. After his individual and congregational prayers, the Sikh takes breakfast and goes to his worldly duty through which he earns his bread for himself and his family. He takes his lunch in the mid-hours.

8. When he returns home from work, he offers evening prayer reciting *Rahiras*, containing nine hymns from the *Adi Granth*, *Chaupai* of Guru Gobind Singh and six stanzas of the *Anand* of Guru Amar Das. He may go to the *Gurdwara* for these prayers.

9. Then he takes his dinner.

10. Before going to bed he has to recite *Sohila* which may be called the bed-prayer.

11. When a Sikh enters a *Gurdwara*, he has to take off his/her shoes and after washing or cleansing his feet he has to

go in the presence of the Guru and bow upto the ground with folded hands in order to show reverence.
12. Every Sikh receives *Karah Prasad*, a mixture of flour, sugar and ghee after the prayer. This *Prasad* is considered a grace from the Lord. This *Karah Prasad* is contributory. One may not contribute at all. One may contribute according to his limits.

Naimittika or obligatory Karmas of a Sikh

1. *Sacraments*—When the child is born, it is taken to the *Gurdwara*, when the mother feels fit and prayers are offered for its long and blessed life. The first letter of the concluding hymn is taken and a name is given to the child after this letter.

The marriage of a young Sikh couple is solemnised by circumambulating around the *Guru Granth Sahib* four times with the *Kirtan* of the four *padas* of a hymn of Guru Ram Das giving description of *lavan*.

When a person dies, prayers are offered for the soul of the departed one. The *Ramkali Sad* of Sundar is read on the concluding day. The ashes are immersed in a nearby river.

Karah Prasad is offered on all occasions and *Anand* of Guru Amar Das is recited.

Sometimes continuous recitation of the *bani* of Guru *Granth Sahib* (*Akhand Path*) is arranged. This recitation is finished in 48 hours. The recitation of seven days excluding nights is *Saptah*.

2. *The Holy Nectar*—The Sikhs may be divided into two types: (1) *Sehjdharis*: who do not grow long hair and do not adopt the discipline of five *K*'s instituted by Guru Gobind Singh (2) *Singhs* or *Khalsa*: They grow long hair and remain under a discipline throughout their life. Their discipline begins with their initiation into *Khalsa* brotherhood. This baptism or initiation ceremony is called *Amrit Chhakna* (the drinking of the holy nectar). Five selected Singhs from a congregation who are ideal Sikhs and follow the discipline strictly and who are called five *beloved ones* perform this ceremony. They offer prayers and recite all the *banis* of *Nitnem* over the vessel in which sugar (in the form of *Patashas*) is mixed in water. The spirit of the *bani* goes into the mixture transforming it into the holy nectar. This nectar is distributed to the Sikhs adopting

the discipline of five *K*s. All the disciples drink it from the same vessel when the hymns from *Guru Granth Sahib* are chanted. This nectar is also sprinkled on their bodies. In this way the disciple drinks deep the spirit of purity and becomes a *Singh* (lion) or a *Khalsa* (God's own).

3. Five *K*s: At this ceremony the disciple is asked to observe *Nitnem* regularly and wear five *K*s: *Kesh* (long hair), *Kachh* (underwear), *Kara* (iron bangle), *Kangha* (the comb) and *Kripan* (the sword). *Keshas* denote saintly appearance, *Kachh* is meant for self-control, *Kara* for abstaining from the use of hand for theft or adultery, *Kangha* denotes cleanliness of mind and body. The significance of *Kripan* is self-defence, but in the times of emergency, it can be used for a right, truthful and just cause.

4. *Taboos*: Any minor offence with regard to the discipline is a taboo for a *Singh*, but the following four are the major ones:

1. He has not to remove hair from any part of the body under any circumstances.
2. He should never eat *Halal* i.e. the meat cut and prepared in the mode adopted by Mohammedans.
3. He should never commit adultery and
4. He should never use tobacco in any form.

Penalty or Tankhah: A Sikh, who makes a confession before the congregation regarding any major or minor offence, a disciplinary action is taken against him by *Sadh Sangat* according to the nature of offence. Since a confession is a sort of repentance, the punishment given is of a mild nature, either the recitation of *bani* or the service of the *Sadh Sangat*.

The Service: The service of *Sadh Sangat*, Khalsa brotherhood or of society is considered a great meritorious act. The Service of the holy congregation in the form of fanning, providing water for drinking and grinding flour for the common kitchen creates humility and other good qualities in the mind of a Sikh.

Langar or a free Common Kitchen: The best service for the brotherhood or society is free kitchen. The institution of free kitchen was started by Guru Nanak at Kartarpur, which was carried forward by other Gurus. Even Emperor Akbar had to partake food in the common kitchen of Guru Amar Das. The

Sikh performs all kinds of service in the common kitchen, He cleanses the used utensils also. In all the major Gurdwaras of the Sikhs, a free kitchen is provided for the poor and the visiting Sikhs.

Holy pilgrimage: The *Gurdwara* is the place of pilgrimage for a Sikh. He visits the historic Gurdwaras. His main purpose for making such journeys is his attendance of congregations at these places and also his desire to meet ideal Sikhs in order to learn more from their experiences in the spiritual domain. For a Sikh there are four thrones (*Takhat*) or seats of authority:

1. Shri Takhat Amritsar.
2. Shri Takhat Patna Sahib.
3. Shri Takhat Keshgarh Sahib, Anandpur.
4. Shri Takhat Hazur Sahib, Nanded.

The Head priests of these *Takhats* are considered authorities on Sikh Religion. They themselves are saints, soldiers and scholars.

Hukamnama and Gurmatta: An order from the *Guru* to the *Sangat* of a particular area or an individual is known as *Hukamnama*. The recitation of a hymn from the *Adi Granth* is considered an order from the *Guru*, therefore, it is also called *Hukm*. A resolution passed by the holy congregation for the welfare of the community is called *Gurmatta*. Such *Gurmattas* passed originally at *Akal Takhat* were considered as orders for all the Sikh ranks.

Panth: A Sikh is a constituent of the *Panth*. The word *Panth* means the path or the distinct Religion. An order for the *Panth* is meant for every individual Sikh. This order can only come from the Guru or the holy congregation meeting at *Akal Takhat*.

When a Sikh meets a Sikh, he has to greet him with the following words:

Wahiguru Ji ka Khalsa

Wahiguru ji ki Fateh

"The Khalsa belongs to God and the Victory is of God"
The war-cry of the Sikhs is Sat Sri Akal, *i.e.* "The Timeless is Truth."

God Realization

The chief objective of human life is considered God-realization by the Sikh Gurus.[176] The human body is the only medium* through which this objective can be fulfilled.[177] The human body is the temple of God. It is a microcosm. It is sheer wastage of time to search for God outside the body.[178] Our body is primarily the abode of our soul. The Higher Soul or God is hidden within this soul. Unless we know our soul fully well, it is impossible to know God.

Our soul is our 'self.' Our body is one of its outer covering. In itself the 'self' is a luminous non-elemental substance which is a part and parcel of Brahman. The curtain of illusion cannot be lifted without knowing the 'self.'[179]

But how can we know our self? The self can be known with the help of the *Guru*. Guru Nanak says:

Every one praises himself, he wants self-aggrandisement.
The self cannot be realised without the *Guru*, nothing occurs from speaking or listening.
If one realizes the Word, his ego will melt away.[180]

Sri Raga, M. I.

The annihilation of ego and recitation of the Name of the Lord brings the realisation of the self.

Whosoever realises the self realises God, just as the tree of nectar will bear further the fruit of nectar. Whosoever tastes this fruit of nectar realises the truth.[181] In order to know, the seeker has to imbibe all the good qualities and virtues. Guru Amar Das says:

Whosoever realises the self, he knows all the qualities.[182]

Maru Solha, M. III.

The qualities or virtues form the foundation on which can be raised a spiritual edifice. With these qualities the self shines like a mirror in which the Higher Soul manifests itself. Without the qualities the body is like a dead mass.[183] Without

---

*This idea is found in *Tantras* also: "There is no birth like unto the human birth. Both *Devas* and *Pitris* desire it ... Human birth is the stepping stone to the path of liberation." *Vishvasara Tantra* as quoted in *Studies in the Tantras and Veda* by Shri M. P. Pandit.

the qualities one falls into the dirt of *maya* and ego and experiences births and deaths repeatedly;[184] the pearls of qualities lie latent in the sea of the body. A true disciple, finds them out.[185] A true disciple is a buyer of qualities. He never forgets the pure Name of the Lord,[186] but the purchaser of qualities is rarely seen.[187] Guru Amar Das says:

> Gather together the qualities so that the vices may go away
> They may be absorbed by the Word of the perfect Guru
> Whosoever is the purchaser of qualities, he knows the qualities
> He recites the Word, the Name, which is nectar.
> Whosoever gathers the qualities, I bow before him
> Sing the praises of the Lord at His door.[188]   *Asa*, M. III.

Thus the Word of the *Guru* is the chief requisite for God-realization. It concentrates the mind on the Pure Lord and brings in purity. When the mind becomes absolutely pure, the Lord enters it. There is Union of the Lord (Brahman) and the lady (Soul).

The selfless action (*Karma*), devotion (*Bhakti*) and knowledge (*Gyan*) put us on the right pathway, because the Grace of the Lord begins at the very outset and the resultant is God-realization. The *Guru* gives us knowledge, the word given by him creates devotion and selfless action. By the Grace of the Lord we meet the *Guru* and by the Grace of the *Guru* we meet the Lord. The *Guru* says:

> The abode of the inaccessible beauty is in the mind (heart)
> Rarely one recognises it with the Grace of the Guru
>   *Gauri*, M. V.
> There is unending treasure in this cave.
> Where lives *Hari*-the Unknowable. Unfathomable.
> Whoever seeks him outside the body
> Cannot attain the Name and experiences great misery . . .[189]
>   *Majh*, M. III

The mystic experiences an ecstatic mood in which he finds himself face to face with the Lord:

> The invisible. inaccessible, the Unknowable and the Pure Lord is seen by the disciple with his own eyes.[190]
>   *Sri Raga Ki Var*, M. IV. Pauri

But this ecstatic mood is the resultant of our devotion towards the Lord by feeling continuously his lotus-feet in our heart. In this way the light dawns and the mystic meets the Lord.[191]

The mystic is aware of the Divine beauty. In his earlier adventures he remains in the company of the good. He realises that the path of God can be known only from the saints.[192] In the company of the saints he listens to the praises of the Lord and with the maturity of this state of *Shravan* he enters the next state of *Mannan i.e.* putting faith in whatever he has listened. He who listens and puts faith enters the abode of the Self.[193] His primal need is satisfied and thus he rises above all other worldly needs.[194] With full faith he concentrates on the Lord (*Niddhyasan*) and this state brings the mystic face to face with the Lord. Guru Arjan says:

With the Grace of the saint my wishes have been fulfilled
With his grace I have realised the treasure of qualities.
There is calmness and comfort in my mind.
There is light of crores of suns, saith Nanak.[195]

Todi, M.V.

The States of God-realization is known as *Sehj*. Guru Amar Das says about this state:

O Brother! we cannot attain *Sehj* without the *Guru,*
With the *WORD* it dawns, *Hari* or Truth is realised.
When one is misled, the study of scriptures or their narration is useless.
The *Sehj* is in the fourth state, the true disciple experiences it.[196]

Sri Raga, M. III

Sehj is not realised by actions and illusion is not cast away without *Sehj.*
Sehj is realised by the Grace of the *Guru* and in this way the illusion is removed, saith Nanak.[197]

Ramkali, M. III Anand

The State of *Sehj* is also known as the fourth state or *Chautha Pad,* Supreme state or *Param Pad.* It is called fourth state because it is beyond the other three states *i.e.* Awakening (*Jagrit*), dream (*Svapan*) and dreamless sleep (*Sushupti*), it is also beyond the ken of three qualities of *Rajas, Tamas* and *Sattva*, which are the components of *maya* (*Anjan*). A mystic realises the Pure Lord (*Niranjan*) in this world of impure *maya* (*Anjan*). But this realization is not an easy task. The seeker has to abandon lust, anger, falsehood calumny, *maya*, ego, sex, woman, attachment, pride, love of son and wife and worldly wants (*trishna*). He has to concentrate on the Lord and has to lose himself in the Word.[198]

God-realization has been depicted metaphorically as the blossoming of the lotus. The lotus of the heart which lies withered in a downward direction turns up and blossoms forth. Guru Arjan says;

> By remembering the feet of the Lord, the Upside down lotus hath blossomed,
> God Himself hath appeared. This is the saying of the saints.[199]
>
> *Gauri Bawan Akhri*, M.V.

Whosoever realises God, has none else in his heart except God. He remains attuned to the Will of the Lord. He is in *sehj*, contentment and without any desire.[200] A person who realises Brahman in this world is *Jivan Mukta*. He is a *Brahm Giani* (Knower of Brahman). When he leaves this world, his soul is merged in the Lord as a ray merges in the sun or a drop of water merges in the ocean.[201] The state of God-realization can never be explained as a dumb person can never describe the relish of the sweets.[202]

There are some obstacles in the way of God-realization and the remembrance of the Name of the Lord. These obstacles are idleness, worldly thoughts, sleep and the power to perform miracles. The Guru has cautioned the disciple about these ills.[203]

The Union of the soul and Higher Soul is known as *yoga* in Indian philosophy. The Sikh view of *yoga* has been explained in the chapter entitled, "The Concept of *Yoga*." Just as a lotus remains undefiled in the water, the devotee remains undefiled by *maya*. He crosses the ocean of the world by concentrating on the Lord with the help of the Word,[204] remaining non-attached with the world. He enters 'So Dar'—that door or tenth door—and meets the Lord. Here he listens to the continuous flow of music (*Anahat Sabda*).

The concept of *Nirvana* in Sikhism is different from that of other Indian religions. The true Sikh has no desire to enter heaven. He even discards *Mukti* as defined in Shastras.[205] He wants to remain always at the feet of the Lord, filled with extreme devotion and love. The extreme devotion of the disciple does not make him mad and senseless, but inspires him for nobler action and attainment of higher knowledge.

God-realization is the result of both effort and Grace. Guru Nanak has talked of five regions (*khand*), in this connection, the first being the region of piety and the last that of truth. The seeker is born in the region of piety (*Dharam Khand*), His ideal is the attainment of the region of Truth (*Sach Khand*). The maturity of pious actions leads the seeker to the region of knowledge (*Gian Khand*) in which he becomes aware of the vastness of the universe (the creation of the Lord) and its infinite expanse. With the maturity of knowledge, the seeker enters the region of effort (*Saram Khand*). In this region of beauty, his mind and intellect become super-fine. This brings the seeker to the region of grace (*Karam Khand*), where he attains the necessary spiritual strength in order to enter that last region *i.e.* the region of truth (*Sach Khand*). In this region the Journey of the seeker comes to an end. He realises Truth *i.e.* God. Thus piety becomes the basis of God-realization.

NOTES AND REFERENCES

[1]काएिंग्रउ देवल — पीपा
[2]जो ब्रह्मिं डे सोई पिंडे — पीपा
[3]सुचु होवै त सचु पाईऐ — आसा दी बार
[4]मन जीतै जग जीत — जुपजी
[5]सदा रहै कंचन सी काएिंग्रा काल न कबहू बिआपै । — शबद हजारे पातशाही १०
[6]सो तनु निरमलु जितु उपजै न पापु । — गौड़ो म. ५
[7]रैणि गवाई सोइ कै दिवसु गवाएिंग्रा खाइ ।
हीरे जैसा जनमु है कउडी बदले जाइ । — गोड़ी सहला १
[8]कबीर मानस जनमु दुलंभ है हीएि न बारे बार ।
जिउ वन फल पाके भुएि गिरहि बहुरि न लागहि डार । — सलोक कबीर
[9]इस देही कउ सिमरहि देव । — भैरउ कबीर
[10]लख चउरासीह जोनि सवाई । माणस कऊ प्रभि दीई वडिआई ।
वस पउड़ी ते जो नर चूके सौ आइ जाइ दुखु पाएिदा । — मारू म. ५
[11]जब लगु जरा रोगु नहीं आएिंग्रा ।
जब लगु कालि ग्रसी नही काएिंग्रा । — भैरउ कबीर
[12]अबर जोनि तेरी पनहारी — आसा म: ५
[13]खात पीत खेलत हसत बिसथार । — गोड़ी म: ५
[14]दुलभ देह पाई वडभागी । — गोड़ी म: ५
[15]विस खाधी ततकाल मर जाइ — वार गोड़ी २ म: ४

NOTES AND REFERENCES 113

16रो गुदारु दोवे बुझे ता वेंदु सुजाणु ।   महला २-वार-माझ
17वैदा वेंद सुवेंद तू पहिला रोगु पछाण ।
ऐसा दारु लोड़ि लहू जितु वंझे रोगा घाणि ।
जितु दारु रोग उठिअहि तनि सुखु वसै ग्राइ ।
रोगु गवाएिअहि ग्रापणा त नानक वेंदु सदाए ।   मः २ वार मलार
18हउमै दीरघ रोग है   वार ग्रासा मः १
19खसमु बिसार कीए रस भोग । ता तठि उठि खलोए रोग ।   मलार मः १
20मिठ रस खाए सु रोगि मरीजै.. ..   भैंरउ मः १
21सुखहु उठे रोग पाप कमाएिग्रा ।   वार माझ मः १
   रोगहु रोग सु ग्रंति विगोवै ।   मारु मः १
   रोगी कउ दुखु रोण विश्रापै ।   बसंत मः १
22ग्रधिक सुश्राद रोग ग्रधिकाई   मलार मः १
23जैसा बितु तैसा होए वरतै ग्रपुना बलु नही हारै ।   धनासरी मः ५
24किटु ग्रवेहा जीविग्रा जितु खाए वधाएिग्रा पेटु   मः १, वार सूही
25भूखे भगति न कीजै ।   सोरठि कबीर
26ग्रंन न खाए देही दुख दीजे   रामकली मः १
   ग्रंन न खाएिग्रा सादि गवाएिग्रा   वार ग्रासा मः १
27ग्रंन पाणी थोड़ा खाएिग्रा ।   वार ग्रासा मः १
28बाबा होरु खाणा खुसी खुम्रार ।
   जितु खाधै तनु पीड़ीऐ मन महि चलहि विकार ।   सिरी राग मः १
29कउण मास कउण सागु कहावै किसु महि पाप समाणे ।   वार मलार मः १
30एितु मदि पीतै नानका बहुते खटीग्रहि बिकार   वार बिहागड़ा मः १
31दुरमति मदु जो पीवते बिखलोपति कमली ।
32जितु पीनै मति दूर होए बरलु पवै विचि ग्राए ।
   आपणा पराएिग्रा न पछाणई खसमहु धके खाए ।
   जितु पीतै खसमु विसरै दरगह मिले सजाए ।
   झूठा मदु मूलि म पीचई जेका पार वसाए ।   मः ३ वार बिहागड़ा
33फरीदा पिछल राति न जागिग्रोहि जीवदड़ो मुएिग्रोहि   सलोक फरीद
34दातन नीति करेिए   तनखाह नामा
35उठि एिसनानु करहु परभाते   बसंत मः ५
36बिन एिसनान न भोजन खावै ।   गुरु प्रताप सूरज ३, ४३
37करि एिसनानु सिमरि प्रभु ग्रपना मन तन भए ग्ररोगा ।   सोरठि मः ५
38कुरबाणी तिना गुरसिखां पिछल राती उठि बहंदे ।
   कुरबाणी तिना गुरसिखां ग्रंम्रित वेले सर नहावंदे ।   माई गुरदास, वार १२
39ग्रलप ग्रहार सुलप सी निंद्रा   पातशाही १०
40काम क्रोध काएिग्रा कउ गाले   रामकली मः ४
41घालि खाए किछु हथहु देए   वार सारंग महला १
42नामा कहे तिलोचना मुखि ते राम समालि ।
   हाथि पांउ कर काम सर चीति निरंजन नालि ।   सलोक कबीर
43हरि कीरतनु सुणे हरि कीरतनु गावै ।

तिसु जन दुख निकटि नहीं आवै ॥ गौड़ी महला ५

⁴⁴जोग न खिंथा जोग न डंडे जोग न भसम चड़ाईऐ ।
जोग न मुंदी मूड़ मुडाईऐ जोग न सिंङी वाईऐ । ...
जोग न बाहर मड़ी मसाणी जोग न ताड़ी लाईऐ ।
जोग न देस दिसंतर भविऐ जोग न तीरथ नाईऐ । ... सूही म: १
⁴⁵अंजन माहि निरंजन रहीऐ जोग जुगति इव पाईऐ । सूही म: १
⁴⁶एक द्रिसटि कर समसर जाणे जोगी कहीऐ सोई । सूही म: १
⁴⁷गली जोग न होई ..... सूही महला १
⁴⁸मित्र सत्र सम एक समानें जोग जुगति नीसाणी । गूजरी महला ५
⁴⁹एहु जोग न होवै जोगी जि कुटंब छोड परिभवण करहि ।
                                               रामकली असटपदी म: ३
⁵⁰हाटी बाटी रहै निरालम रूख बिरख उदिआने ।
कंद मूल आहारो खाईऐ अउधू बोलै गिआने । सिध गोसटि-रमकली म: १
⁵¹जैसे जल महि कमल निरालम मुरगाई नैसाणे ।
सुरति-सबद भवसागर तरीऐ नानक नाम वखाणे ।
                                               सिध गोसटि-रामकली म: १
⁵²गुर मन भारिओ कर संजोग । अहिनिस रावै भगति जोग ।
गुरु संत सभा दुख मिटे रोग । जन नानक हरिवर सहिज जोग । बसंतु महला १
⁵³गुरु का सबद मनहि महि मुंद्रा खिंथा खिमा हुंढावउ ।
जो किछु करै भला कर मानउ सहिज जोग निधि पावउ । आसा महला १
⁵⁴रसना जपीऐ एक नाम ।
ईहां सुख आनंद घना आगै जीअ के संग काम ।
कटीऐ तेरा अहं रोग । तूं गुरु प्रसादि कर राज जोग । गोड़ी म: ५
⁵⁵कर भेख न पाईऐ ब्रह्म जोग हरि प.ईऐ सत संगती......
                                               कानड़ा महला ४-पड़ताल
⁵⁶मिहर मसीति सिदकु मुसला. ... माझ की वार म: १
⁵⁷... डंडा परतीत । जपुजी
⁵⁸पाखंड भगति न होवई. .... सिरो राग म: ३
⁵⁹भगति करहु तुम सहै केरी जे सहु पिआरे भावए । आसा छंत म: ३
⁶⁰आपणा भाणा तुम करहु ता फिर सहु खुसी न आवए । आसा छंत म: ३
⁶¹भौ बिनु भगति न होवई. ... सूही वार ३
⁶²हरि भगत हरि का पिआ रहे. .... सिरी राग महला ३
⁶³जिस अंतरि प्रीति लगै सो मुकता ।
इंद्री बस सच संजम जुगता ।
गुरु कै सबद सदा हरि धिआए एहा भगति हरि भावणिआ ।
                                               माझ असटपदी म: ३

⁶⁴भगत करहि मूरख आप जणावहि ।
नच नच टपहि बहु दुख पावहि ।

नचिएँ टपिएँ भगति न होई ।
सबदि मरैं भगति पाइ जन सोइ ।   गौड़ी महला ३
⁶⁵भगत जना कउ रखदा अपणी किरपा धार ।   सिरी राग म: ५
⁶⁶भाई रे भगति हीण काहे जग आइआ ।   सिरी राग म: ३
⁶⁷भगति भाव एहु मारग बिखड़ा गुर दुआरै को पावए ।   आसा छंत म: ३
⁶⁸होर कितै भगति न होवई बिन सतिगुर कै उपदेस ।   सिरी राग म: १
⁶⁹आइ पइआ तेरी सरणाई ।
जिउ भावै तिउ लेहि मिलाई ।
कर किरपा प्रभ भगती लावहु
सच नानक अंम्रित पीए जीउ ।   माझ म: ५
⁷⁰गुर की मति तूं लेहि इआने । भगति बिना बहु डूबे सिआने ।
हरि की भगति करहु मन मीत । निरमल होइ तुमारो चीत ।
                                                गौड़ी सुखमनी महला ५
⁷¹नानक बिन भगती जग बउराना साचै सबदि मिलाई ।   आसा म: ३
⁷²एक भगति भगवान जह प्रानी कै नाहि मन ।
जैसे सूकर सुआन नानक मानो ताहि तन ।   सलोक महला ९
⁷³गोबिंद गोबिंद गोबिंद संग नामदेव मन लीना ।
आढ दाम को छीपरो होइओ लाखीणा ।
बुनना तनना तिआगि कै प्रति चरन कबीरा ।
नीच कुला जोलाहरा भइओ गुनी गहीरा ।
रवदास ढबंता ढोर नीत तिन तिआगी माइआ ।
परगट होआ साधू संगि हरि दरसन पाइआ ।
सैन नाई बुतकारीआ ओहु घर घर सुणिआ ।
हिरदै वसिआ पारब्रह्म भगतां महि गणिआ ।
एह बिधि सुनि कै जाटरो उठि भगती लागा ।
मिले प्रतख गुसाईआ धंना वडभागा ।   आसा धंना
⁷⁴मोह मलिन नींद ते छुटकी कउन अनुग्रहि भइओ री ।
महां मोहनी तुध न विआपै तेरा आलस कहां गइओ री ।
सुर नर देव असुर त्रैगुनीआं सगलो भवन लुटिओ री ।
दावा अगन बहुत त्रिण जारे कोई हरिआ बूट रहिओ री ।
काजर कोठि महि भई न कारी निरमल बरन बनिओ री ।   आसा म: ५
⁷⁵महां मंत्र गुर हिरदै बसिओ अचरज नाम सुनिओ री ।
कर किरपा प्रभ नदर अविलोकन अपने चरन लगाई ।
प्रेम भगति नानक सुख पाइआ साधू संग समाई ।   आसा म: ५
⁷⁶भगति भंडार गुरबाणी लाल ।
गावत सुणत कमावत निहाल ।   आसा म: ५
⁷⁷बिन गुर गुण न जापनी बिन गुण भगति न होइ ।   सिरी राग म: ३
⁷⁸सतिपुरख जिन जानिआ सतिगुर तिसु का नाउ ।   गौड़ी सुखमनी म: ५
⁷⁹वाएनि चेले नचनि गुर । पैर हिवाएनि फेरनि सिर ।

उड उड राखा झाटे पाईं । वेखैं लोक हसहि घरि जाईं ।
रोटीआं कारनि पूरहि ताल । आपु पछाड़हि धरती नाल ।

आसा दी वार म: १

⁸⁰नानक अंधा होईं कै दसे राहैं सभ मुवाए साथैं ।
⁸¹साहिब जिस का नंगा भुखा होवैं तिसदा नफर किथों रज खाए ।

वार माझ महला १

वार गौड़ी १-म: ४

⁸²गुरु ईसर गुरु गोरख बरमा गुरु पारबती माई ।

जपुजी

⁸³सेवहु सतगुरु समुंद अथाहा ।

मारू सोलहे म: १

अंमृतसर सतगुरु सतवादी जितु नातैं कऊआ हंस होईं ।

गूजरी म: ४

सतिगुर बोहिथ हरिनाम है ....

सिरी राग म: ४

.... गुरु खेवट सबद तराइआ राम ।

बिहागड़ा छंत म: ४

गुरु पारस मिलिऐं कंचन होए .....

आसा असटपदी म: ३

सतगुरु साह सिख वणजारे ।

आसा असटपदी म: १

आप बीचारै सु परखे हीरा । एक द्रिसटि तारे गुरु पूरा ।

ऐसा साहु सराफी करे । साची नदर एक लिव तरे ।

आसा असटपदी म: १

भूले मारग जिनहि बताएआ । ऐसा गुरु वडभागी पाएआ ।

बिलावल महला ५

मन कुंचर पीलक गुरु .....

वार गूजरी १-महला ३

मेरा बंद गुरु गोविंदा .....

सोरठ म: ५

ढाठी भीत भरंम की भेटत गुर सूरा ।

आसा छंत म: ५

जैंसा सतगुरु सुणीदा तैंसो ही मैं डीठ ।
विछुड़िआ मेलैं प्रभु हरि दरगहि का बसीठ ।

वार रामकली २-महला ५

⁸⁴अपरंपर पारब्रह्म परमेसुर नानक गुरु मिलिआ सोई जीउ ।

सोरठ म: १

आदि अंत एको अवतारा । सोई गुरु समझीओ हमारा ।

चौपई पातशाही १०

⁸⁵बाणी गुरु गुरु है बाणी विचि बाणी अंमृत सारे ।
गुरबाणी कहैं सेवक जन मानैं प्रतख गुरु निसतारे ।

नट असटपदी म: ४

⁸⁶सबद गुरु सुरति धुन चेला .. : .

रामकली म: १

⁸⁷ब्रह्मा बिंदैं सो सतगुर कहीऐं .....

मलार म: ४

⁸⁸सतगुरु सभना दा भला मनाईदा ...

वार गौड़ी १-महला ४

⁸⁹सतगुरु धरती धरम है ....

वार गौड़ी ४-म: ४

⁹⁰सतगुरु अंदरहु निरवैर है सम देखैं ब्रह्म इक सोईं ।

वार गौड़ी १-म: ४

⁹¹सुखदाता दुख मेटणा सतगुरु असुर संघार ।

सिरी राग असटपदी म: ४

⁹²जिसु मिलिऐं मन होईं अनंद सो सतगुरु कहीऐं ।

गौड़ी म: ४

⁹³गुरु दाता गुर हिवैं घर ....

माझ वार १

⁹⁴सतगुरु सचा साहु है सिख दे हरि रासे ।

आसा छंत म: ४

⁹⁵सतिगुरु बोहिथ हरि नाम है ....

सिरी राग महला ४

गुरदेव दाता हरिनाम उपदेसे ।

गौड़ी बावन अखरी म: ५

⁹⁶गुरदेव माता गुरदेव पिता गुरदेव सुआमी परमेसुरा ।
गुरदेव सखा अगिआन भंजन गुरदेव बंधप सहोदरा ।

गौड़ी बावन अखरी म: ५

⁹⁷सतगुरु हथ कुंजी होरत दर खुलैं नाही

तर पूरै भाग मिलावणिआ ।	माझ असटपदी महला ३
गुर कुंजी पाहू निवल . . .
अवरि न कुंजी हथ ।	वार सारंग-सलोक महला २
[98]कुंभे बधा जलु रहै जल बिनु कुंभु न होइ ।
गिआन का बधा मनु रहै गुर बिनु गिआनु न होइ ।	ग्रासा दी वार महला १
[99]छल नागनि सिउ मेरी टूटनि होई ।
गुरि कहिआ एह झूठी ढोही ।
मुखि मीठी खाई कउराइए ।
अंमृत नाम मन रहिआ अघाइए ।
लोभ मोह सिउ गई विखोटि ।
गुरि क्रिपालि मुहि कीनी छोटि ।
एह ठगवारी बहुत घर गाले ।
हम गुरि राख लीए किरपाले ।
काम क्रोध सिउ ठाटु न बनिआ ।
गुरि उपदेसु मुहि कानी सुनिआ ।
जहि देखउ तहि महा चंडाल ।
राख लीए अपने गुरि गोपाल ।
दस नारी मैं करी दुहागनि ॥
गुरि कहिआ एह रसहि बिखागनि ।
इन सनबंधी रसातलि जाइए ।
हम गुरि राखे हरि लिवलाए ।
ब्रहमेव सिउ मसलति छोडी ।
गुरि कहिआ एहु मूरखु होडी ।
एहु नीघर घर कही न पाए ।
हम गुरि राख लीए लिवलाए ।
आए प्रभू पहि अंदरि लागि ।
करहु तपावसु प्रभु सरबागि ।
प्रभ हरि बोले कीने निआंए
सगल दूत मेरी सेवा लाए ।
तूं ठाकुरु एहु ग्रिहु सभु तेरा ।
कहु नानक गुरि कीआ निबेरा ।	प्रभाती असटपदी महला ४
[100]गुर की मूरति मन महि धिआनु ।
गुर कै सबदि मंत्र मनु मान ।
गुर के चरन रिदै लै धारउ ।
गुर पारब्रहु सदा नमसकारउ ।१। रहाउ ।
भूले कउ गुर मारगि पाइआ । अवर तिआगि हरि भगती लाइआ ।
जनम मरन की त्रास मिटाई । गुर पूरे की बेअंत बडाई ।२।
गुर प्रसादि उरध कमल बिगास । अंधकार महि भइआ प्रगास ।
जिनि कीआ सो गुर ते जानिआ । गुर किरपा ते मुगध मनु मानिआ ।३।
गुरु करता गुरु करणै जोग । गुरु परमेसरु है मी होगु ।

कहु नानक प्रभि एहै जनाई । बिनु गुर मुकति न पाईऐ भाई ।४।   गोंड महला ५

¹⁰¹बीज मंत्र सरब को गिग्यान । चहुं वरना महि जपै कोऊ नाम ।
                                                            गउड़ी सुखमनी म: ५
¹⁰²हरि के नाम समसर किछु नाहि ।   गौडी सुखमनी
¹⁰³भरीऐ मत पापा कै संग । ओह धोपै नावै कै रंग ।   जपुजी
¹⁰⁴कहिते पवित सुणते पवित . . . . .   सिरी राग छंत महला ५
¹⁰⁵पारजात एहु हरि को नाम । कामधेनु हरि हरि गुण गाम ।
                                                            गोड़ी सुखमनी म: ५
¹⁰⁶सरब धरम महि स्रेशट धरम । हरि को नाम जपु निरमल करम ।
                                                            गौड़ी सुखमनी म: ५
¹⁰⁷जह मात पिता सुत मीत न भाई । मन ऊहा नामु तेरे संग सहाई ।
जह महा भइआन दूत जम दलै । तह केवल नामु संगि तेरे चलै । . . .
अनिक माएिग्रा रंग तिख न बुझावे । हरि का नामु जपत आधावे ।
                                                            गौड़ी सुखमनी म: ५
¹⁰⁸राम नाम बिन सांति न आवै जप हरिनाम सु पार परें ।   मैरउ महला १
¹⁰⁹संसार रोगी नाम दारू मैल लागे सच बिना ।   धनासरी म: १
¹¹⁰अंमृत बेला सचु नाउ वडिआई बीचारु ।   जपुजी
¹¹¹ऊठत बैठत सोवत ध्रिआईऐ । मारग चलत हरे हरि गाईऐ ।   आसा महला ५
¹¹²कारज काम बाट घाट जपीजै । गुर प्रसादि हरि अंमृत पीजै ।   आसा महला ५
¹¹³नामा कहै तिलोचना मुख ते रामु समालि ।
हाथ पाउ करि कामु सम्ं चीतु निरंजन नालि ।   सलोक कबीर
¹¹⁴कबीर सुपनै हू बरडाएि कै जिह मुख निकसै रामु ।
बाके पग की पानही मेरे तन को चामु ।६३।   सलोक कबीर
¹¹⁵हउमै नावै नालि विरोधु है दुऐि न वसहि इक ठाऐि ।   वडहंसु महला ३
¹¹⁶लख मड़िग्रा कर एकठे एक रती ले भाहि ।   आसा म: १
गुरमुखि कोटि उधारदा भाई लै नावै एक कणी ।   सोरठि म: ५
¹¹⁷सूरबीर धीरज मति पूरा । सहिज समाधि धुनि गहिर गंभीरा ।
सदा मुकति ता के पूरन काम । जा के रिदै वसै हरि नाम ।
सगल सूख आनंद अरोग । समदरसी पूरन निरजोग ।
आऐि न जाऐि डोलै कत नाही । जा कै नाम बसै मन माही ।
                                                            रामकली महला ५
¹¹⁸रामनाम बिन बिरथे जग जनमा   भैरउ महला १
¹¹⁹अब मुहि जलत राम जल पाएिग्रा । राम उदक तन जलत बुझाएिआ ।
                                                            गोड़ी कबीर
आतसु दुनीआ खुनक नाम खुदाएिग्रा ।   वार मलार महला १
¹²⁰ईकदु जीमो लख होहि लख होवहि लख बीस ।
लखु लखु गेड़ा आखीअहि एकु नामु जगदीस ।
एतु राहि पति पवड़ीआ चड़िऐ होऐि ईकीस ।   जपुजी
¹²¹मनहु कमावै मुख हरि हरि बोलै । सो जन इत उत कतहि न डोलै । गोड़ी म: ५
¹²²राम राम सभ को कहै कहिऐ राम न होऐि ।

NOTES AND REFERENCES 119

गुरप्रसादी राम मन वसै ता फल पावे कोई ।   गूजरी म: ३
[128]मुखहु हरि हरि सभ को कहै विरलै हिरदै वसाएिआ ।
नानक जिनकै हिरदै वसिआ मोख मुकृति तिन पाएिआ ।   वडहंस महला ३
[124]मनुमख हरि हरि कर थके मैल न सकी धोएि ।
मन मैले भगति न होवई नाम न पाएिआ जाए ।   सिरी राग महला ३
[125]बिनु जिहवा जो जपै हिआएि । कोई जाणै कैसा नाउ ।   मलार म: १
[126]गुरमुखि रोमि रोमि हरि धिआवै ।   रामकली सिध गोसटि महला १

[127]सतसंगत कैसी जाणीऐ । जियै इको नाम वखाणीऐ ।   सिरी राग म: ५
[128]सची संगत बैसणा सचनाम मन धीर ।   सिरी राग म: ३
[129]ऊतम संगत उतम होवै । गुण कउ धावै अवगुण धोवै ।   आसा असटपदी महला १
[130]सभ की रेन होएि रहै मनूआ सगले दीसहि मीत पिआरे ।   आसा महला ५
[131]महा पवित्र साधु का संग । जिस भेटत लागै प्रभु रंग ।   आसा महला ५
[132]पिंगुल परबत पारि परे खल चतुरब कीता ।
अंधुले त्रिभवण सूझिआ गुर भेटि पुनीता ।१।
महिमा साधु संग की सुनहु मेरे मीता ।
मैलु खोई कोटि अघ हरे निरमल भए चीता ।१। रहाउ । . . .
सिंधु बिलाई होए गएिओ तिनु मेरु दिखीता ।
स्रमु करते दम आढ कउ ते गनी धनीता ।   बिलावलु म: ५
[133]पारस भेट कंचन धातु होएि सत संगत की वडिआई ।   गूजरी असटपदी महला १
[134]सची संगत सच मिलै सचे नाएि पिआर ।   वार वडहंस म: ३
[135]नाव रुप भएिओ साधू संग भवनिधि पार परा ।   जैतसरी म: ५
[136]बुधि प्रगास प्रगट भई उलट कमल बिगसना ।
सीतल सांति संतोख होएि सभ बूझी त्रिसना ।   बिलावलु महला ५
[137]दहदिस धावत मिट गए निरमल थान बसना ।   बिलावलु म: ५
[138]हरि के जन ऊतम जग कहीअहि जिनि मिलिआ पाथर सेन ।   कानड़ा म: ४
[139]बिसर गई सभ तात पराई । जब ते साधू संगति मोहि पाई ।   कानड़ा म: ५
[140]ना को बैरी नही बिगाना सगल संग हम कउ बनि आई ।   कानड़ा महला ५
[141]हरि गुन ऊच नीच हम गाए गुर सतगुर संग सखे ।
जिउ चंदन संग बसै निंम बिरखा गुन चंदन के बसखे ।   नट म: ४
[142]सतसंगत सतगुरु चाटसाल है जित हरि गुण सिखा ।   वार कानड़ा महला ४-पौड़ी
[143]कबीर मारी मरउ कुसंग की केले निकटि जु बेरि ।
उह झूलै उह चीरीऐ साकत सगु त हेरि ।   सलोक कबीर
[144]कबीर चंदन का बिरवा भला बेड़िउ ढाक पलास ।
ओए भि चंदनु होएि रहे बसे जु चंदन पासि ।   सलोक कबीर
[145]कबीर बांस बडाई बूडिआ इउ मत डूबहु कोएि ।
चंदन कै निकटे बसे बांसु सुगंधु ना होएि ।   सलोक कबीर
[146]कबीर संत न छाडै संतई जउ कोटिक मिलहि असंत ।
मलिआगुरु भुयंगम बेढओ त सीतलता न तजंत ।   सलको कबी
[147]आगिआ भई अकाल की तबीचलाएिओ पंथ

सब सिखन कउ हुकम है गुरु मानीओ ग्रंथ ।
गुरु ग्रंथ जी मानीओ प्रगट गुरां की देह ।
जाका हिरदा सुध है खोज सबदि महि लेहि ।
148कीरतनु निरमोलक हीरा । आनंद गुणी गहीरा ।   रामकली म: ५
149चरणार बिंद भजनं रिदयं नाम धारणह ।
कीरतनं साध संगेण नानक नह द्रिसटंति जमदूतनह ।   सलोक सहस क्रिती म: ५
150हरि कीरति भगति अनंदु है सदा सुखु वसै मनि आए ।   सारंग वार ४-म: ४
151हरि कीरतनु आधारु निहचल एहु धनो ।   आसा म: ५
152हरि कीरतनु करह हरि जसु सुणहि तिसु कवला कंता ।   सोरठि वार ४-पउड़ी
153वैर विरोध मिटे तिह मन ते । हरि कीरतनु गुरमुख जो सुनते ।
                                                                       गोड़ी बावत अखरी महला ५
154हरि कीरतनु भगत नित गांवदे हरि नाम सुखदाई ।   गोड़ी वार ४-म: ४
155हरि कीरतनु ताको आधारु । कहु नानक जिसु आप दएिआर । भैरउ म: ५
156सो किछु कर जितु मैलु न लागै ।
हरि कीरतन महि एहु मनु जागै ।   गौड़ी म: ५
157जे लोड़िह सदा सुखु भाई । साधू संगति गुरहि बताई ।
ऊहा जपीऐ केवल नाम । साधू संगत पारगराम ।
सगल तत महि तत गिआन । सरब धिआन महि एकु धिआनु ।
हरि कीरतन महि ऊतम धुना । नानक गुर मिल गाएि गुना ।   बसंतु महला ५
158हरि कीरतन गाबहु दिनु राती सफल एहा है कारी जीउ ।   माझ म: ५
159मन माहि चितवउ चितवनी उदमु करउ उठि नीत ।
हरि कीरतन का आहरो हरि देहु नानक के मीत ।   गूजरी वार ५
160जागत जोत जपै निस बासुर एक बिना मन नैक न आनै ।
पूरन प्रेम प्रतीत सजै ब्रत गोर मड़ी मठ भूल न मानै ।
तीरथ दान दीआ तप संजम एक बिना नहि एक पछानै ।
पूरन जोत जगे घट महि तब खालस ताहि निखालस जानै ।   सवयं पातशाही १०
161भूखे भगति न कीजै । यह माला अपनी लीजै ।
हउ मागउ संतन रेना । मैं नाही किसी का देना ।
माधो कैसी बनै तुम संगे । आपि न देहु त लेवउ मंगे ।
दुइ सेर मागउ चूना । पाउ घीउ संगि लूना ।
अध सेर मांगउ दाले । मोकउ दोनउ वखत जिवाले ॥
खाट मांगउ चउपाई । सिरहाना अवर तुलाई ।
ऊपर कउ मांगउ खींधा । तेरी भगति करै जनु बींधा ।
मैं नाही कीता लबो । इकु नाउ तेरा मैं फबो ।
कहि कबीर मनु मानिआ । मनु मानिआ तउ हरि जानिआ ।   सोरठि कबर
162गोपाल तेरा आरता ।
जो जनु तुमरी भगति करंते तिनु के काजु सवारता ।
दालि सीधा मागउ घीउ । हमरा खुसी करै नित जीउ ।
पनीआ छादनु नीका । अनाजु मगउ सत सी का ।

गऊ भैंस मगऊ लावेरी । इक ताजनि तुरि चंगेरी ।
घर की गीहनि चंगी । जनु धंना लेवै मंग।   धनासरी धंना

143तेरे भाणे सरबत का भला ।   श्ररदास
164राजा तखत टिकै गुणी भै पंचाएिण रत ।   मारू महला १
तखति राजा सो बहैं जो तखतु लाएिक होई ।   बार मारू महला ३
165बाझहु वाजब माल दे होर न हाकम लेिए ।
नानक श्राखै रुकनदीन हाकम कहीश्रहि सेिए ।   गौशटि मके मदीने की
166सौ किउ मंदा आखीऐ जितु जंमहि राजानु ।   आसा दी वार महला १
167लोक वेद गुण गिआन विच अरध सरीरी मोखु दुआरी ।
गुरमुख सुखफल निहचउ नारी ।   भाई गुरदास
168सतीआ एह न श्राखीश्रन जो भड़िआ लग जलंन ।
नानक सतीआ जाणीश्रन जि बिरहे चोट मरंन ।   वार सूही म: ३
. . . .भी सो सतीआ श्राखीश्रन सील संतोख रहंन ।   वार सूही म: ३
169एका नारी जती होेिए . . . . . .   भाई गुरदास
170गरीबा उपर जो खिंजहि दाहड़ी ।
परब्रह्म सा श्रगन महि साड़ी ।   गोड़ी महला ५
171गुर सतिगुर का जो सिखु श्रखाए सु भलके उठि हरि नामु धिआवै ।
उदमु करे भलके परभाती इसनानु करे श्रमृतसर नावै ।
उपदेसि गुरु हरि हरि जपु जापै सभि किलविख पाप दोख लहि जावै ।
फिरि चड़ै दिवसु गुरबाणी गावै बहदिआ उठदिआ हरिनामु धिआवै ।
जो सासि गिरासि धिआए मेरा हरि हरि सो गुरसिख गुरु मनि भावै ।
जिसनो दएिश्रालु होवै मेरा सुश्रामी तिसु गुरसिख गुरु मनि भावै ।
जनु नानकु धूड़ि मंगे तिसु गुरसिख की जो श्रापि जपै अवरह नाम जपावै ।
     गोड़ी वार ४-म: ४
172गुरमुखि नामु दानु एिसनानु । गुरमुखि लागे सहजि धिआनु ।
गुरमुखि पावै दरगह मानु । गुरमुखि भउ भजनं परधानु ।
गुरमुखि करणी कार कराए । नानक गुरमुखि मेल मिलाए ।३६।
     सिध गोसटि म: १
173गुरमुख मिठा बोलणा जो बोलै सोई जप जापै ।
गुरमुख श्रखी देखणा ब्रह्म धिआन धर आप सु श्रापै ।
गुरमुख सुणना सुरति कर पंच सबद गुरु सबद श्रलापे ।
गुरमुख किरत कामवणी नमसकार डंडउत सिंझापै ।
गुरमुख मारग चलणा परदखणा पूरन परतापै ।
गुरमुख खाणा पहनणा जग भोग संजोग पछापै ।
गुरमुख सवण समाधि है श्रापे आप न थाप उथापै ।
घरबारी जीवन मुकत लहिर नहीं लब लोभ विश्रापै ।
पार पए लंघ वरै सरापै ।   भाई गुरदास वार ६ पोड़ी १८

174हरि बिनु अवर क्रिया बिरथे ।   गौड़ी म: ५
175अंमृत बेला सचु नाउ वडिआई वीचारु ।   जपुजी

¹⁷⁶सो जीविग्रा जिस मन वसिग्रा सोए । नानक अवर न जीवै कोए ।
जो जीवै पत लथी जोए । सभ हराम जेता किछु खाए । वार माझ म: १
नानक सोई जीविग्रा जिन इक पछाता । वार गोड़ी २-महला ५
काहे रे बन खोजन जाई ।
सरब निवासी सदा अलेपा तोही संग समाई ।
पूहप मध जिउ बास वसत है मुकर माहि जैंसे छाई ।
तैंसे ही हरि बसै निरंतर घट ही खोजहु भाई । धनासरी म: ६
¹⁷⁷सरीरहु भालण को बाहर जाए ।
नाम न लहै बहुत वेगार दुख पाए ।
मनमुख अंधे सूझै नाही ।
फिर घर आए गुरमुख वथ पावणिआ । माझ असटपदी म: ३
¹⁷⁸सभ किछु घर महि बाहर नाही ।
बाहर टोलै सो भरम भुलाही ।
गुरपरसादी जिनी अंतर पाइग्रा ।
सो अंतर बाहर सुहेला जीउ । माझ महला ५
¹⁷⁹जन नानक बिन आपा चीनै मिटै न भ्रम की काई । धनासरी म: ६
¹⁸⁰सभ सालाहै आप कउ वडहु बडेरी होए ।
गुर बिन आप न चीनीऐ कहे सुणे किग्रा होए ।
नानक सबद पछाणीऐ हउमे कहै न कोए । सिरी राग असटपदी म: १
¹⁸¹जिनी आतम चीनिआ परमातम सोई ।
एको अमृत बिरख है फल अमृत होई ।
अमृत फल जिनी चाखिग्रा सच रहे अधाई ।
तिना भरम न भेद है हरि रसन रसाई । आसा असटपदी म: १
¹⁸²आप पछाणे सो सभ गुण जाणे । मारू सोलहे म: ३
¹⁸³बिन गुण काम न आवई ढहि ढेरी तन खेह । सिरी राग म: १
¹⁸⁴गुण विहूण माइग्रा मलधारी ।
बिन गुण जनम मूए अहंकारी । आसा म: ४
¹⁸⁵सरीर सरोवर गुण परगट कीए ।
नानक गुरमुख मथ ततु कढीए । आसा म: ४
¹⁸⁶गुणकारी गुण संग्रहै अवरा उपदेसेन ।
सो वडभागी जि ओना मिल रहे अनुदिन नाम लएन । सूही असटपदी म: ३
¹⁸⁷गुण का गाहक नानका विरला कोई होए । वार मारू १-महला ३
¹⁸⁸गुण संग्रहु विचहु अउगण जाहि ।
पूरै गुर कै सबद समाहि ।
गुण का गाहक होवै गुण जाणे ।
अमृत सबद नाम वखानै ।
जो गुण संग्रहै तिन बलिहारै जाउ ।
दर साचे साचे गुण गाउ । आसा म:
¹⁸⁹अगम रूप का मन महि थाना ।

गुर प्रसादि किनै विरलै जाना ।१। गोंडी म: ५
इसु गुफा महि अखुट भंडारा ।
तिसु विचि वसै हरि अखल अपारा ।
... ...
सरीरहु मालणि को बाहरि जाए ।
नामु न लहै बहुतु वेगारि दुखु पाए । माझ महला ३
[190]अदिसटु अगोचरु अलखु निरंजनु सो गुरमुखि देखिआ आखो ।
सिरी राग को वार महला ४-पोड़ी
[191]चरन कवल रिद अंतरि धारे ।
अगनि सागर गुरि पारि उतारे । गोंडी म: ४
[192]मेरो सुंदरु कहहु मिले कित गली ।
हरि के संत बतावहु मारगु हम पीछै लागि चली । देवगंधारी म: ४
[193]जिन सुण कै मंनिआ तिना निज घर वासा । सिरी राग म: ३
[194]जिनी सुण सिखा गुरु मंनिआ तिना भूख सभ जावी । तिलंग म; १
[195]संत प्रसाद मेरे पूर मनोरथ कर किरपा भेटे गुणतास ।
सांति सहिज सूख मन उपजिओ कोटि सूर नानक परगास । टोडी म: ५
[196]भाई रे गुरु बिन सहिज न होइए ।
सबदे ही ते सहिज उपजै हरि पाइआ सच सोइ ।
पड़ीऐ गुणीऐ किआ कथीऐ जा मूढहु घुथा जाइ ।
चउथे पद महि सहिज है गुरमुख पलै पाइ । सिरी राग असटपदी म: ३
[197]करमी सहिज न ऊपजै बिण सहिजै सहसा ना जाइ । ...
कहै नानक गुरपरसादी सहिज ऊपजै एह सहसा इव जाइ ।
रामकली अनंदु म: ३
[198]परहरि काम क्रोध झूठ निंदा तजि माइआ अहंकार चुकावै ।
तजि कामु कामिनी मोहु तजै ता अंजन माहि निरंजनु पावै ।
तजि मानु अभिमानु प्रीत सुत दारा तजि पिआस आस राम लिव लावै ।
नानक साचा मनि वसै साच सबदि हरि नामि समावै । वार माझ १-म: ४
[199]चिति चितवउ चरणारबिंद ऊध कवल बिगसांत ।
प्रगट भए आपहि गोबिंद नानक संत मतांत । गोंडी बावन अखरी म: ५-सलोक
[200]प्रभ मिलणे की एह नीसाणी ।
मनि इको सचा हुकमु पछाणी ।
सहजि संतोखि सदा त्रिपतासे अनंदु खसम कै भाणे जीउ । माझ म: ५
[201]सूरज किरण मिली जल का जल हूआ राम । बिलावल म: ५
[202]जिनु चाखिआ तिसु आइआ सादु ।
जिउ गूंगा मन महि बिसमादु ।
आनद रूपु सभु नदरी आइआ ।
जन नानक हरि गुण आखि समाइआ । बिलावलु म: ५
[203](क) प्रभ मिलबे की लालसा ता ते आलस कहा करउ री । आसा म: ५
(ख) वस आणिहु वे जन इस मनु कउ मत बासे जिउ नित भउदिआ । सूही म: ४

(ग) हउ किउ कंत पिआरी होवा । सहु जागे हउ निस भर सोवा ।
                                                                        आसा म: ५

(घ) रिधि सिधि सभ मोहु है नामु न वसै मन आए ।
                                                                        वार वडहंस म: ३

²⁰⁴सुरति सबदि भव सागर तरीऐ नानक नामु वखाणै ।
                                                                सिध गोसटि रामकली म: १

²⁰⁵मुकति बपुड़ी भी गिआनी तिआगै।
                                                                        मारू म: ५

Index

Adharma, 5
Adi Granth, 1, 3-12, 14, 16-20, 26-27, 30, 32-39, 43-44, 60, 62, 79, 85-86, 101, 103-4, 107
Agamas, 85
Agami, 45
Agni, 34
Ahamkara, 28, 33-34, 54, 56-57
Ahimsa, 45
Ahriman, 20
Ahura Mazda, 20
Ajapa Jap, 93
Ajiva, 5
Akal Takhat, 107
Akash, 5, 34
Akbar, 106
Akhand Path, 105
Al-Boraq, 36
Amar Das, Guru, 15, 41, 60, 80, 82, 100, 104-6, 108-10
Amrit Chhakna, 105
Amrit Vela, 90, 103
Anahat Sabda, 111
Anand, 32, 104-5
Anandmaya Kosha, 25
Anand Sahib, 104
Andaj, 36
Angad, Guru, 55, 57, 101

Anjan, 110
Annamaya Kosha, 25, 57
Antarang Bhakti, 82
Anuraga Bhakti, 82
Apas, 34
Arambhvada, 37
Aranayaka, 4
Archan, 83
Arhats, 5
Arjan, Guru, 1, 3, 5-6, 32, 44, 52, 56-58, 76, 78-81, 83, 87, 92, 94, 96-97, 101, 110-111
Artha, 99
Asa Ki Var, 104
Asan, 81
Asanas, 8
Asatkaryavada, 37
Ashramas, 2, 4, 7, 12, 99
Atam-gunas, 7
Atam-nivedan, 83
Atman, 4-5
Aum, 4, 16-18
Avataras, 7
Avidya, 26, 29, 38, 84

bani, 14, 41, 86, 95, 105
bania, 105
behrang bhakti, 82

Beni, 39-40
Bhagats, 61
Bhagavat Gita, 5, 79
Bhakta, 14
Bhakti, 5, 82-83, 96
Bhakti cults, 7
Bhakti Movement, 1, 5, 81
Bhakti yoga, 79-81, 83
Bhani, 46
Bhutadi, 33
Bija mantra, 89-90
Body, gross, 60
Body, subtle, 60
Brahm, 16, 18
Brahma, 18-19, 35, 85
Brahmacharya, 17
Brahman, 4, 8, 10-11, 13, 16-23, 26, 28-29, 31-32, 35, 37-38, 43, 81, 86, 89-90, 108, 111
Brahmana, 4
Brahmin(s), 2, 4, 8, 24
Brahm Giani, 45, 101, 111
Brahmparinamavada, 11, 38
Brahm Yoga, 81
Brhadaranayakopanishad, 17, 45
buddhi, 25, 33
Buddhists, 4-5

cause and effect, law of, 46
causation, physical law of, 77
Charvakas, 4, 44
chaudeh bhavan, 36
Chaupai, 104
chautha pad, 18, 110
Chitra Gupta, 61
cittavrittinirodha, 79
common Kitchen, 106
Concepts—Brahman, 16-22; Jiva, 22-26; Maya, 26-29; Creation, 29-38; Microcosmic Theory, 38-42; Karma and Transmigration, 42-45; Hukm, 45-48; Grace, 49-50; Virtue and Vice, 50-54; Ego, 54-56; Mind and Intellect, 56-59; Death and Life after Death, 59-62; Health, 76-79, Yoga, 79-81; Bhakti, 82-84; Sat-guru and Name, 84-93; Sadh Sangat and Kirtan, 93-97; A true Sikh and an ideal society, 97-102; God-realization, 108-12
Conscious Power, 46

darshan, 104
Das Bhav, 83
Dasam Granth, 14
daswandh, 99
Death, 59
Devas, 108
devotion, 52, 54, 84, 96, 109
dewans, 93
Dhanna, 83, 98-99
Dharam Khand, 14, 112
Dharma, 5, 13, 49, 51, 54, 81, 98-99
dhyana, 81, 88
Divine Will, 46
drinks, 78
duties, 54
dvijas, 2
Dynasts, 46

Education, 58
ego, 12, 54-56, 77, 108-10
Egyptian, 44

Farid, 1, 3, 61

Gabriel, 36
Ganapatyas, 2
gandha, 34
Gian Khand, 14, 112
Gobind Singh, Guru, 1, 85-86, 97
godly qualities, 53
god of Justice, 62
God-realization, 108-12
gods, 7, 9, 62, 76; Gorakhnath, 40, 80
goshtas, 79
Grace, 12, 49
Grahasthya Ashrama, 7
Granth, 59
Granth Sahib, Guru, 14, 95, 103-6
Greeks, 44
Gurmatta, 107

INDEX

Gunas, three, 11, 13, 21, 27-28, 31, 34-35, 43
Gurdas, Bhai, 15, 78, 101; Gurdwara(s), 95, 103-5, 107
Gurmat Philosophy, 15
Gurmukh, 6, 48, 101-2; Guru, 84-86, 94, 96, 101, 108-9
Guru-bani, 86, 96
Guru-soul, 86
Gyan, 109
Gyan Yoga, 79, 81

Hala, 106
Hardy, Thomas, 46
Hargobind, Guru, 15, 101
Hari, 97
Hari Kirtan, 79
Hathyoga, 2, 79, 80
Hathyogis, 79
health, physical and mental, 78
heaven, 13-14, 43, 61
hell, 13-14, 43-44, 61
Higher Soul, 108
Hindu, 1
Hindu culture, 5
Hinduism, 8, 20, 36
Hindu Philosophy, six systems of, 5
Hindu Shastras, 103
Hindu society, 4
Hindu Thought, 19
Hukm, 45-48, 107
Hukmnama, 107

ideal company, 93
ideal society, 93, 97
Indian culture, 4-6, 10
Indian thought, 85
individual, 50-52, 54, 82, 97
individual self, 50
inference, 10
injunctions, 52
intellect, 56, 58
intoxicants, 52, 78
Ishvara, 10, 15, 18-19, 52, 86, 90
Islam, 20, 36
Islamic culture, 2

Itihasas, 5

jada, 36
jaidev, 1, 3, 14
jainism, 5
jains, 4, 5
janeu, 7
Jap Sahib, 104
Japji, 14, 29, 33, 35-36, 57, 92, 103-4
Jarayuja, 36
Jiva(s), 5, 10-11, 18, 22-23, 25-29, 42, 45, 47, 49, 52-54, 56-57, 59-60, 80
jivam-mukta, 101, 111
jivatman, 57, 59
Jupji—see *Japji*

Kabir, 1-2, 4-5, 8, 14, 43, 60-61, 83, 91, 95, 98-99
kachh, 106
Kal, 5
Kalchakrayana, 40
Kaliyuga, 52, 97
Kama, 99, 109
Kamadhenu, 90
kangha, 106
kany, 55
kara, 106
karah prasad, 104
karam kanda, 42, 112
karam khand, 14
karma, 5, 12-13, 19, 42-44
karma, and transmigration, 4, 61
karmas, 13, 42-45, 49, 51, 77, 103
karma Yoga, 79, 81
Karma Yogi, 7
Kartarpur, 106
Kathopanishad, 16, 57
Kesh, 106
Khalsa, 15, 97, 105, 106
Khalsa brotherhood, 106
khand, 112
khani, 36
kirtan, 83, 96-97, 104-5; Kripan, 106
Kritayuga, 97
Ks, 106
Kshatriyas, 4, 24

Langar, 106
laukika Bhakti, 82
lavan, 105
lila, 10, 31, 38
Lokayatas, 44

Macrocosm, 12, 38-41, 76
Madhava, 98
Mahabharata, 5
Mahabhutas, 33-35
Mahakal, 15, 88
Mahat, 33-34, 57
manas, 33
Mandukyopanishad, 17
manomaya kosha, 25, 57
mannan, 110
mantra(s), 2, 4, 84, 87-89
Manu Smriti, 54
Mardana, 97
Maya, 10-14, 26, 28-29, 31-32, 35, 43, 56, 84, 87, 109-10, 111
Maya Shakti, 27
Mayavada, 26
means of knowledge, 10; microcosm, 12, 38, 40-41, 76, 108
middle path, 51
mind, 56
mitrata, 83
model man, 101
moksha, 99
monotheist, 2
moral code, 51
Muhammad, 20
mukti, 61, 111
Mul mantra, 16, 19, 29, 89
murti, 88
Muslim, 2, 82
Muslims, 21, 46
Muslim Theology, 46

Nachiketas, 16
Naimittika karmas, 103, 105
nama-rupa, 27
Namdev, 1, 4, 8, 14, 37, 83, 91, 99
Name (of the Lord), 13-14, 56, 61, 80, 84, 86, 90-94, 103, 108-9
Nam Yoga, 80, 92

Nanak, Guru, 1-3, 5-9, 11, 13-14, 1, 35-36, 38-39, 46, 52, 55-56, 58, 608, 77-80, 83, 85-86, 97, 101, 104, 106, 112
Nasadiya Sukta, 4, 30, 35
Nath cult, 2
Nath Yogis, 41
Naudha Bhakti, 83
Nav Khand, 36
Niddhyasan, 110
Niranjan, 110
Nirguna, 10, 18, 27
Nirvana, 57, 83, 111
Nitnem, 103-5
Nitya Karmas, 103
Niyama, 81; noose, 59
Nyaya, 37

padas, 105
pad-sewan; 83; Panch Shabda, 102
Panth, 95, 107; Pap, 43
Para Brahm, 18
Para Brahman, 90
Parinamvada, 37
Parjat, 90
Param pad, 56, 110
Para vidya, 2, 59
Patanjali, 79, 81
patashas, 105
Pauranic, 32, 35, 37; Peepa, 38-39
penalty, 106
perception, 10; pitris, 108
planes, physical, mental and spiritual, 50
Plato, 96, 100
polygamy, 100
polytheist, 2; Pradhan, 33
Prajna, 17
Prakriti, 11, 21, 23, 29, 32-34, 38
Pranamaya kosha, 25
Pranayama, 8, 81, 93
Pran Sangli, 39
prarabdha, 45
Prashnopanishad, 17
Pratyahara, 81
Pravritti marga 99
Prema Bhakti, 83

INDEX

pretender, 85
Prithvi, 34
Prophet, 46
Ptolemy, 36
Pudgal, 5; Puja, 88
punya, 43
Purana(s), 5, 31, 33, 35, 44
Purusha, 4, 11, 21, 23-24, 30, 32-33, 42
Purva Mimansa, 43

qualities, 52, 84, 108-9
Quran, 31, 46

Rahiras, 104
Raja Yoga, 80-81
rajas, 11, 28, 110
Ramanuja, 11, 32, 38
Ramayana, 5
Ramdas, Guru, 58, 81, 101, 105
Ramkali Sad, 105
rasa, 34
Ravidas, 1, 2, 4, 83
Regions, five, 112
reincarnation, 44
Rigveda, 26, 30, 35
ritualism, 51
rupa, 34

sabda, 34; Sach Khand, 14, 112
Sadh(s), 94-95, 101, 103
sadhaka, 41
Sadh Sangat, 13, 54, 93-97, 104, 106
Saguna, 11, 19, 27
Sahajayana, 40
Saint-poets, 85
Saints, 94
Samadhi, 81; Samkhya, 34-35, 37-38,
Samkhyan, 11, 29, 32, 56, 79
Samitis, 4; *Samskara,* 7
Sanatana Dharma, 6
Samchit, 45
Sangat, 94; *Sanjam,* 77
Sannyasi, 2, 7; *Sant,* 95, 101
Saptah, 105; *Saram khand,* 14, 57, 112
Satan, 51; *Sat,* 95
Satguru, 84-85, 101

Sati, 100
Satkaryavada, 37
Satsang, 93
Sattva, 11, 28, 110; *Sauryas,* 2
scriptural testimony, 10
Sehj, 61, 91, 110
Sehjdharis, 105
Sehj Yoga, 80
self, 108
self-mortification, 56; senses, five, 51, 77-78
service, 106
Shabad Brahm, 90
Shaivas, 2, 21
Shaktas, 2
Shakti, 29
Shankaracharya, 37-38
Shastras, 88, 92, 111
Shastic injunctions, 51
sheaths, 25
Shiksha Guru, 89
Shiva, 1, 8, 19, 35, 85; *Shravan,* 110
Shudra, 2; *siapa,* 61
Siddha, 57
Siddh Goshta, 79-80
Siddhi, 88-89
Sikh(s), 21, 43, 52, 78-79, 93, 97, 101, 107
Sikh brotherhood, 97
Sikh ceremonies, 102
Sikh Ethics, 103
Sikh Gurus, 40, 51-52, 54, 59, 61, 77-78, 81-83, 85, 97, 100, 106, 108
Sikhism, 1, 51, 79-80
Sikh Philosophy, 3, 10
Sikh Prayer, 58
Sikh Religion, 3, 76, 78, 107
Sikh scriptures, 13, 19, 31
Sikh society, 97
Sikh Thought, 49, 85
Simran, 83
Sin, 13
Singh, 105-6
Society, 54, 97, 100
So Dar, 111
Soedaja, 36

Sohila, 104
soul, 60
soul, Higher, 60
sravan, 83
sthula sarira, 60
sparsha, 34
State, 99, 100
Sukhmani, 31, 33-34, 92, 94, 101
Sunn (Sunya) Samadhi, 10, 30
Surt-Shabad Yoga, 80
Sushupti, 110
Swayyas, 104

Taboos, 106; Taijasa, 17, 33
Taittiriya Upanishad, 90
Takhat, 107
Tamas, 11, 28, 110
Tankhah, 106
Tanmatra, 33-34
Tantra(s), 40, 85, 88, 108
Tantric doctrine, 41
Tantric Sadhana, 40
Tantrikas, 41
Ten Gurus, 86
Theosophists, 44
Thinking Principle, 46
Thrones, 107
Tithe, 99
Tradition, 85
Transmigration, 44-45
Trigunatita, 27
Trilochan, 8, 45, 91
Trimurti, 35
Triratna, 5
Trishna, 45, 111
Trumpp, Dr. 85
Turiya, 17-18, 25

Udbhija, 36
untouchability, 8
Upanayana Samskara, 7

Upanishad(s), 2, 4, 16, 85
Unpanishadic Thought, 33
Utopia 97

Vaikarika, 33; Vaisheshika, 37
Vairagi, 24
Vaishnavas, 2, 20
Vaishvanara, 17
Vanaprastha, 7
Vanaprasthi, 2
vandana, 83
vani, 96
Varnas, 12, 99
Varnashrama Dharma, 2
Vayu, 34
Vedanta, 2, 38
Vedas, 2, 4, 85
Vedic Dharma, 6
vice(s), 50, 51, 53
Vijnanamaya kosha, 25, 57
vikaravartin, 27
virtue(s), 13, 50, 51, 53
Vishnu, 18-19, 35, 85
Vishvasara Tantra, 88, 108
Vi artavada, 37

Wahi(u) guru, 21, 90
Woman, 100
Word, 14, 86, 89

Yama, 13, 16, 59-60, 81, 91, 96
Yoga(s), 2, 79-81, 83, 111
Yoga Darshana, 81
Yoga Shastra, 37
Yoga system, 79
Yogi(s), 56, 80, 99; Yogic terminology, 40
Yogini Tantra, 88
Yagis, 76-77
Yugas, 32